Courtyard and
Terrace Gardens

A Wisley Gardening Companion

Courtyard and Terrace Gardens

ROBERT PEARSON, GEORGE PRESTON,
JACK ELLIOTT and RAY WAITE

Cassell

The Royal Horticultural Society

THE ROYAL HORTICULTURAL SOCIETY

Cassell Educational Limited
Villiers House, 41/47 Strand
London WC2N 5JE
for the Royal Horticultural Society

This compilation copyright © Cassell/the Royal
  Horticultural Society 1993

Gardening in a Small Space copyright © Robert
  Pearson 1980, 1986
Climbing and Wall Plants copyright © George Preston
  1973, 1986
Growing Dwarf Bulbs copyright © Jack Elliott 1988
Gardening in Ornamental Containers copyright © Ray
  Waite 1987

First published 1993

British Library Cataloguing in Publication Data
A catalogue record for this book is available from the
British Library

ISBN 0-304-32044-7

Photographs by Jack Elliott, John Garey, Michael
Jefferson-Brown, Pat Johns, Photos Horticultural,
George Preston, Robert Preston, Martyn Rix, Harry
Smith Collection, Peter Stiles

Phototypesetting by RGM Associates, Southport

Printed in Hong Kong by Wing King Tong Co. Ltd.

Page 1: Bulbs and pansies make a valuable contribution to
this spring display by a front door
Page 2: A variety of shapes, sizes, heights and colours merge
together in this mixed border of a country terrace garden

Contents

Overleaf: This patio garden shows how much colour and interest can be created within a small space

Foreword

The first Wisley Handbooks, published in 1972, launched this most successful series, which has sold more than a million copies to date. From the beginning they have identified the subjects of most interest to the gardener. They originated as articles and lectures delivered to the Royal Horticultural Society, reprinted from the RHS *Journal*. One of the first pamphlets, *Hardy and Semi-Hardy Annuals in the Open Air*, sold for 2d. in 1915. Many of these early leaflets advised gardeners on wartime needs.

With the support and involvement of RHS staff as well as many other excellent authors, the Handbooks have always given clear and concise practical advice, ensuring their success. The first Handbooks were 24 pages, stapled, with black and white illustrations. Now there are more than 60 Handbooks, each of 64 pages and illustrated in colour.

This volume, *Courtyard and Terrace Gardens*, brings together four of the Handbooks, *Gardening in a Small Space*, *Climbing and Wall Plants*, *Growing Dwarf Bulbs* and *Gardening in Ornamental Containers*. It provides in readily available form information and advice on planning and planting these often small, but imaginative, gardens.

No space is too small for a garden, for even a tiny paved area can produce colour blendings and plant associations to be enjoyed throughout the year. Climbing and wall plants help shape a garden by adding individuality and colour to the walls of the garden, as well as those of house, garage or shed. Dwarf bulbs are well suited to a small area and give good value through their freedom of flowering and ease of cultivation. The large and choice range, most readily obtainable and inexpensive, include those suitable for every position. Ornamental plants grown in containers, too, are indispensable to the gardener with limited space and resources. They create points of interest, providing colour, texture and form to furnish the hard surfaces of steps and terraces and enhance the green uniformity of lawns.

This volume carries forward the aims of the early Handbooks, to interest and inform.

Christopher Brickell,
Director General,
The Royal Horticultural Society

Gardening in a Small Space

ROBERT PEARSON

A Mediterranean-style garden well suited to a sunny,
protected courtyard

Introduction

Planning and planting a small garden can be an exhilarating experience. But which plants are best suited for the purpose, and what can they be expected to contribute? It is the purpose of this section to explore the possibilities. Our views on size are naturally coloured by our own circumstances. To the owner of broad acres a garden of one acre in extent might well be considered a small garden. To the owner of a small courtyard garden almost anything might seem large. The title of this section is intended to cover gardens ranging from patio proportions to something not far short of the size of the typical suburban garden.

Paradoxically, gardens which fall into this category can be more difficult to develop successfully than those of more ample proportions: if you reduce the area involved, plant shapes and sizes, colour blendings and plant associations all take on added significance. More thought needs to be given to the integration of both related and disparate features, with plants being used with more discernment and subtlety. If this sounds a little daunting it is not meant to be. The greatest assets you can have when embarking on this kind of venture are an instinctive feeling for plants and the kind of resourcefulness and imagination which most gardeners can "pull out of the hat" when the occasion demands.

Pansies such as the Roggli Giant mixture can contribute colour from spring to the end of summer

Like everybody else whose life has revolved around gardening and plants, I have my own ideas on garden design. To some of these I give an airing now, but I am not a garden designer and for a wealth of excellent and succinct advice on this specialised area I would suggest that you consult another book in this series, *Making a Small Garden*.

My advice to any intending garden maker is to "hasten slowly". Rush into things too quickly and it is easy to make bad mistakes, whether you are coping with the development of a new plot or converting an existing garden to meet your interests and tastes. Get the feel of it, soak up the atmosphere and take note of the surroundings immediately beyond your boundary line before even starting to make a plan or buying-in plants to get things moving.

A prime need is to establish at a very early stage the kind of growing medium you have at your disposal. Even in a small garden there can be considerable variations, so find out the pH rating* of the soil over the area generally and, if necessary, improve the physical structure by digging in peat or composted bark fibre.

As to finding the right home for plants in which you are especially interested, if these have clearly defined needs, then it is important to get the measure of your garden's microclimate; that takes a while. Naturally, one can gather quite a lot straight away, but I would want to know more before I settled on a home for, say, a genista or carpeting helianthemums, which need lashings of sunshine, or, in the case of perennials, for hostas, pulmonarias, hellebores or spindly-stemmed, dainty epimediums, all of which prefer a lightly-shaded position.

Never let your heart rule your head by introducing to the garden plants which are plainly unsuited to the conditions which can be offered. It is so easy to do, and quite unnecessary with the vast range of plants available.

One of your priorities should be to evaluate every vertical surface with a plant bed at its base, to assess its possibilities as a growing area, not only for true climbers but for other shrubs which are so well suited for (or need) such positions—the ceanothuses, chaenomeles, *Cotoneaster horizontalis*, *Chimonanthus*

* The symbol pH is used to denote the chemical reaction of the soil. A neutral soil has a pH of 7.0. Below 7.0 is acid, and above alkaline.

praecox, pyracanthas, and the winter-flowering jasmine (*Jasminum nudiflorum*). By gardening upwards in this way you are automatically increasing your growing area and, by varying the levels of interest, adding immeasurably to the attractions of the garden. Sunny, sheltered walls also provide the right conditions for plants of borderline hardiness which one could not contemplate growing elsewhere; for instance, a high proportion of the ceanothuses.

In all but the smallest gardens—which may well be given over to paving interspersed with plant beds and containers—I would always find room for a lawn, however small. Well-tended grass makes a marvellous foil for other features, and even a wide strip (if that is all that can be accommodated) can greatly enhance the appearance of associated features. It soothes the eye in summer and provides colour in winter.

Shrubs are the backbone of the modern garden—easy to look after and an attraction the year round if you plant with a fair degree of skill, taking size into account.

Against this framework of shrubs, trees and taller-growing conifers are the plants which give the garden its distinction and strongest sense of personality. This is true of even quite small trees. By providing focal points of attention and changes in elevation they perform an indispensable service. Only the most minute of gardens should be devoid of them altogether.

For providing a wealth of interest in relatively small areas of ground the bulbous flowers, the herbaceous perennials, the annuals and biennials are invaluable. They can be used to beautify odd corners of the garden and provide a succession of interest around the year.

Vegetables and fruit most certainly come into the reckoning, too; but only in the most space-effective ways. So far as vegetables are concerned, it makes sense to concentrate mostly on salad and reasonably short-term crops of other kinds, and, in fruits, on trained forms of top fruits and, of course, most types of soft fruits; all come in for discussion later. But now back to more general considerations. Earlier, I made the point about using plants with subtlety. Flowers are at the centre of garden enjoyment, but, leaving aside the roses and a handful of other plants, they are in bloom for a relatively short period. That is accepted, but it makes one think more deeply about the advantages which fine-foliaged plants offer the gardener not over-blessed with growing space. They supplement most marvellously the floral displays either for some six months of the growing season or as a permanent feature in the case of the evergreens. Nor is it only a question of colour; shapes and textures can also give a great deal of pleasure. To whet

14

your appetite just think of the contribution which can be made by the evergreen *Elaeagnus pungens* 'Maculata' ˙ with its gold-splashed leaves, and *Weigela florida* 'Variegata' with its creamy white leaf variegation and soft pink, foxglove-like flowers in May and June, a delightful assemblage of complementary colours.

Perhaps it is almost inevitable, with space at a premium, that over-planting is something which has taken the edge off the beauty of many a small garden. It should be resisted—most of all because the plants won't like it.

Pyrus salicifolia 'Pendula', a delightful tree for the small garden with its weeping habit and silvery leaves (see p. 16)

In Praise of Trees

Trees must be accorded an especially honoured place in gardening, just as in the fashioning of the landscape generally. Beautiful, elegant and imposing are some of the adjectives which come immediately to mind when describing their charms. Some, too, like the birches, are even more beautiful in their leafless winter state. However, with these more than with any other group of garden plants, it is necessary for the head to rule the heart. Trees which will ultimately become far too large for the garden should be discounted from the start.

I'm going to start this brief survey with a selection of trees which provide foliage effects. The first of these is the weeping willow-leaved pear, *Pyrus salicifolia* 'Pendula', one of the loveliest small trees I know with its rounded head and canopy of weeping branches clothed with grey, willow-like leaves giving it an almost ethereal appearance in some lights. It is unlikely to exceed 20ft (6m) in height and is usually nearer 15ft (4.5m) tall. White flowers appear in April. It grows well in all soils of reasonable quality, including those which are heavier, wetter and drier than average.

Very easy-going, too, of course, are the birches of which, alas, most grow too large for the size of garden with which we are concerned. Two which can be used are the well-known *Betula pendula* 'Youngii' (Young's weeping birch) and the narrowly upright growing *B. pendula* 'Fastigiata' which is much less often encountered. Like all the birches (greedy feeders by the way), Young's weeping birch has elegance and style, and makes an excellent focal point in a small garden especially when associated with plants like heathers—the winter-flowering *Erica herbacea* (*E. carnea*) varieties only, if you have a limy soil—which have a natural affinity with it. *Betula pendula* 'Fastigiata', which makes a narrow column 25ft (7.5m) or a little more tall, I've seen used most effectively in a small front garden given over mostly otherwise to lawn.

If you have a garden at the upper end of the size range, the Swedish birch, *B. pendula* 'Dalecarlica', with its pendulous branches bearing light green, deeply cut leaves, could be considered. It is almost certain in time to reach a height of 40ft (12m), but a mitigating factor is that birches, with their airy framework of branches, are not trees which greatly inhibit light.

Not many gardeners, in my experience, seem to be aware of the existence of that charming little weeping willow, *Salix purpurea* 'Pendula', even though it is the one by far the best suited to small gardens. This standard form of the purple osier reaches a height of little more than 9 to 10ft (2.7–3m) and a spread of a few feet less. It is only since the early 1970s that *Robinia pseudoacacia* 'Frisia' has become well known. This golden-yellow-foliaged false acacia creates a glorious splash of colour to a height of some 30ft (9m) right through from spring to autumn, when the colouring changes before leaf fall to a pleasing amber shade. With a width of about 15ft (4.5m) it can, moreover, be incorporated into many a planting scheme. Culturally, it will do well in a wide range of soils, although it must be exposed to plenty of sunshine to bring out the colour at its best. 'Frisia' has, however, a skeleton in its cupboard: its wood is brittle and branch snapping is a common occurrence if one is imprudent enough to plant it in a position where wind can set it creaking and straining. A sheltered position is a necessity.

A tree one links naturally in one's thoughts with the robinia is the thornless *Gleditsia triacanthos* 'Sunburst'. Its size is roughly similar to that of the last mentioned and it is also accommodating culturally. However, it doesn't hold its leaf colour like 'Frisia' and, while the fern-like leaves begin a glorious golden yellow, this gradually changes to pure green as the season advances. On the other hand, it has a rather better shape than the robinia (whose branches can look a little ragged) and it does not suffer from brittle wood. Both trees are tolerant of air pollution.

Only about half the height of the last two—and slow to put on growth— is a very striking sycamore named *Acer pseudoplatanus* 'Brilliantissimum', a gorgeous sight in spring when the leaves open a beautiful shrimp pink, which gradually gives way to greenish-yellow and, finally, to pure green. This needs to be grown in a position where the light will strike it at the right angle. So, too, does the lovely snake-bark maple *A. pensylvanicum*, but only if you can provide it with a lime-free soil. It has beautiful white- and green-striped bark and, for a brief spell in autumn, butter-yellow leaf colouring. Perhaps the best of all the maples for autumn colour, though, is the Japanese maple, *A. palmatum* 'Osakazuki' which assumes at that time brilliant red hues. Like all the *palmatum* varieties, however, it needs a position out of cold winds. Neither of this pair will usually exceed 15ft (4.5m) in height and, like all the maples, they appreciate a rather good, nicely moist but well-drained soil in which to grow.

Most hollies rank as trees rather than shrubs and for year-round display these reliable but rather slow-growers are unsurpassed. My favourite is the male (and therefore non-berrying) *Ilex aquifolium* 'Golden Queen', some 15ft (4.5m) tall and 8 to 10ft (2.4–3m) in width. It shouts out a message of good cheer, especially in winter, with its mass of prickly leaves an amalgam of green and rich golden-yellow (on the margins), with some grey suffusions with the green. Another holly, somewhat smaller growing, is 'Handsworth New Silver', with leaves of green and grey margined with creamy white. When carrying its bright red berries it is very eye-catching indeed. Remember that with female hollies there needs to be a male form growing reasonably close to get a good set of berries.

Turning to flowering trees, it is the ornamental cherries (Prunus) which generally excite the most interest. A whole host of them are suitable for most small gardens, but I must restrict my choice to just a handful. One of the loveliest in my opinion is P. 'Shimidsu Sakura' which, for several weeks in late spring, captivates with its pure white, double flowers (these open from pink-tinged buds). It grows some 12 to 15ft (3.6–4.5m) tall and so can be found a home in many a small space open to plenty of sunshine, which is something that all flowering cherries need. Its shape, too, is beguiling, for it makes a well-rounded head with the lower-most branches sweeping down almost to ground level. A cherry of fully weeping habit is 'Kiku Shidare Sakura', similar in height to the last and with deep pink, double blooms in April.

Where lateral space is not available but height is, a tree is advantageous to the overall design. The natural choice of cherry would be 'Amanogawa' which grows up to 20ft (6m) tall but not more than 8 ft (2.5m) wide and often quite a lot less. This becomes a pillar of shell pink in late April and May. With rather more lateral room, Prunus × hillieri 'Spire' might appeal even more, for this grows up to 25ft (7.5m) tall and up to 10ft (3m) wide bearing soft pink blooms in April and providing really good, rich red leaf colour in autumn.

In the context of this book I would consider the autumn cherry, P. subhirtella 'Autumnalis' well worth your attention, too, for, despite its name, it does bear its small, semi-double white flowers right through from November to March, except when hard weather intervenes. These are very pretty seen as a network of white against the bare branches. It will make a tree of rather spreading habit to 20ft (6m) or so and much the same in height.

The ornamental crabs appeal to me, especially shapely little Malus × robusta in its form known as the Yellow Siberian. This is a profusion of white blossom for a time in spring, and then from early autumn is highly decorative with its long-persisting yellow fruits. Its height and spread is usually well under 20ft (6m). Again, there is a good columnar variety in 'Van Eseltine', which makes a tree some 20ft (6m) tall on which semi-double, shell-pink flowers

Acer palmatum 'Osakazuki', a large bush or rounded small tree, provides a striking splash of colour in autumn (see p. 17)

open from red buds in May and yellow fruits follow in early autumn. Especially beautiful in May, for its pale pink to white flowers opening from rosy red buds, is the Japanese crab *Malus floribunda*, which makes a round-headed tree from 15ft (4.5m) tall and wide.

Likewise, there are numerous excellent mountain ashes (*Sorbus*), which belong to the Aucuparia section of the genus. Quite delightful is *Sorbus vilmorinii*, only 15ft (4.5m) or so tall and less wide, with a neat habit, pretty fern-like foliage and, in autumn, pendent clusters of fruits, which start off red and gradually change to pink and finally white with pink suffusions. Very highly regarded also is the larger 'Joseph Rock' (up to 25ft

[7.5m] tall but considerably less in width) which has fine autumn leaf colour and fruits starting off a rather pale yellow but deepening in colour as they mature.

The flowering cherries, ornamental crabs and mountain ashes all grow well in any average soil (including those of an alkaline nature), given good drainage. The first two need sunny positions, but the last are satisfactorily grown in either sunshine or light shade.

Unquestionably the best magnolia for small gardens is *Magnolia stellata*, to which you will find reference in the chapter on shrubs (see p. 28), but it is impossible to ignore the delightful *M. x soulangeana* which is such a wonderful sight in April when the goblet-shaped blooms, suffused with purple on the outside of the petals and white within, open on the bare branches. And, of course, flowering continues well into May, when the leaves are unfolding. The reservation about it in the practical context is its spread, for it makes a low-branched tree of, perhaps, eventually 25 to 30ft (7.5–10m) tall and as much in width, with the growths coming almost to the ground.

Magnolia x soulangeana and its varieties are, alas, not suitable for limy soils. What suits them best is a good well-drained loamy soil which is retentive of moisture. Don't plant in a frost pocket either or the blooms will suffer. Despite what I have said about their size, *M. x soulangeana* and its forms are often seen as main features in town and city gardens and, as is well known, they have a high resistance to atmospheric pollution.

Let's finish with a broom and a laburnum, namely *Genista aetnensis*, the Mount Etna broom, which is more often grown as a large shrub than a single-stemmed tree, and *Laburnum x watereri* 'Vossii'. Both are much to be valued for bringing strong yellows—the most cheerful of all colours—into the garden at different parts of the summer.

In fact, the Mount Etna broom can be extraordinarily useful if you want to give a planting scheme height without casting much shade. Grown on a clear stem, it will carry its elegant top-hamper of whippy growths to a height of up to 20ft (6m) and be really spectacular when the racemes of golden-yellow pea flowers are borne in July and August. If medium-sized shrubs are grown around its base the rather gaunt appearance of the tree will be entirely masked. Late May and early June is the time when *Laburnum x watereri* 'Vossii' produces its profusion of long, rich yellow racemes of flowers. Expect it to have a height eventually of 30ft (9m) and a width of 20ft (6m). The genista likes full exposure to sunshine and, for preference, a lightish soil. The laburnum will be happy in any average soil in sunshine or light shade.

Key Conifers

Conifers fascinate me. These are plants where shapes, colours and textures so often combine in a specific species or variety to provide us with something having dramatic impact. Keeping within the size limitations imposed by the theme of this book, one need look no further for an example of this than the conical-shaped blue spruce, *Picea pungens* 'Koster', with its tier on tier of branches densely packed with silvery-blue leaves. Eventually, this will reach 30ft (9m) or so in height and perhaps 15ft (4.5m) wide. It's a marvellous associate for heathers and, of course, for growing with others of its kind—conifers which will provide sharp contrasts in form like the prostrate, grey-green *Juniperus horizontalis* 'Bar Harbor', which makes a mass of whippy stems and provides an attractive ground-covering carpet, or maybe a small and slow-growing yew like *Taxus baccata* 'Semperaurea', the yellow of whose foliage varies in intensity from summer to winter and which will not reach its full height of about 6ft (1.8m) for many years.

You will have to decide whether you want to have a conifer which, although not growing very wide (perhaps about 12ft [3.6m]) will in time be nearer 40ft (12m) than 30ft (9m) in height. In certain circumstances it could still have a place in quite a small garden. If that is so, then a golden conifer to consider—for a sunny position, which all yellow-foliaged conifers need to bring out their colour—could be *Chamaecyparis lawsoniana* 'Lanei', which carries its growths in dense sprays and which, while presenting a golden-yellow face to the world, is a greeny yellow underneath. It is especially effective in winter when such warm colours are a real need. Other golden conifers are *Cupressus macrocarpa* 'Goldcrest' (but only for a sheltered position) and *Taxus baccata* 'Fastigiata Aurea', the form of the Irish yew which has green leaves with yellow margins. The first grows eventually to about 30ft (9m), the second to 15ft (4.5m).

You could also be interested in two other Lawson cypresses—*Chamaecyparis lawsoniana* 'Columnaris', which makes a narrow column of glaucous blue, tight-packed, vertical sprays and, after ten years, is unlikely to be more than 8ft (2.5m) tall (and twice that in 20 years), and 'Pembury Blue', raised in a Kent nursery some 40 years ago and popular on the Continent but only now getting into its stride here. 'Pembury Blue' has an attractive conical habit and will probably be about 12ft (3.6m) tall some ten years from planting, although eventually reaching some 30ft (9m) in height. In a small garden, however, such slowness of growth can, quite often, be a decided advantage.

An interesting introduction from the United States which also brings blue into the garden is *Juniperus scopulorum* 'Blue Heaven', pyramidal in habit and eventually around 20ft (6m) tall but only half that height after ten years. If you want the equivalent of an exclamation mark, however, to set off a low planting, then the pencil-slim *Juniperus virginiana* 'Skyrocket' could well be the answer, faster growing than the last and never becoming much over 1 to 2ft (30–60cm) in width, even though its full height can be as much as 20ft (6m). It has greyish blue colouring.

An old friend to many gardeners is *Thuja occidentalis* 'Rheingold', a conifer of conical habit with yellow foliage of a very sympathetic shade (often described by nurserymen as old gold). This turns to a pleasing shade of bronzy gold after the arrival of winter. Much the same old-gold colouring is a winter feature, too, of a beautiful small thuja of Dutch raising—*T. occidentalis* 'Sunkist', which is rich yellow during the summer months. It should prove a popular choice for a sunny position, only a few feet tall after a considerable number of years. 'Rheingold' may eventually reach a height of as much as 10ft (3m), but it is more likely to be 5 or 6ft (1.5–1.8m), and 'Sunkist' perhaps $3\frac{1}{2}$ to 4ft (1–1.2m). For more about some of the best small conifers see the Wisley Handbook *Dwarf and Slow-growing Conifers*.

Pinus mugo, the dwarf mountain pine, is much used in gardens in Switzerland—not unnaturally as it is a native of the mountains of central Europe. A good dwarf form like 'Gnom' is a handsome sight with its characteristic bristly growths of dark green; globe shaped, and taking many years to reach a maximum height and width of 5 to 6ft (1.5–1.8m), it is notably good at coping with limy soils. Another extremely attractive form of the dwarf mountain pine is 'Mops', with a dense, bun-like habit and slow growth. It is usually only about $1\frac{1}{2}$ft (45cm) tall by 2ft (60cm) wide after ten years. Another of small size which could be of interest is a form of the native Scots pine, *Pinus sylvestris* 'Beuvronensis', dome shaped and handsome and with lighter coloured foliage than the last. It will reach much the same size as 'Gnom' (or a little more), again after many years.

As to the growing conditions suitable for the different genera, junipers will grow well in any soil of reasonable quality, including soils of a chalky nature (indeed they are the best conifers for such conditions, followed, perhaps, by the yews, varieties of *Chamaecyparis lawsoniana* and the thujas, although none except the yews are going to take too kindly to really thin soils of this kind). They

Chamaecyparis lawsoniana 'Columnaris' can make a fine feature in a small space

need plenty of exposure to sunshine. The chamaecyparis and cupressus varieties do well in most well-drained soils of average quality, given shelter from cold winds and good light conditions. The cypresses are of variable degrees of hardiness, and *macrocarpa* varieties like the one mentioned can certainly be damaged if exposed to cold, drying winds. They are excellent for growing in seaside districts in more favoured parts of the country. The cypresses also need to be planted young to get them off to a good start.

The yews are very accommodating, both with regard to soils and available light, doing well in sunshine or shade. Chalk soils are taken in their stride by yews, as I've already remarked, and *Taxus baccata* is endemic to such conditions as a British native. Piceas, however, like good, moisture-retentive but well-drained soils and are best kept off very thin, chalky soils. The pines need good light and clean air but will do well on poorish soils and some, like *Pinus mugo*, are very good on limy soils.

23

Hamamelis mollis, witch hazel, seen here in January, flowers from autumn to early spring. The fragrant flowers are frost-resistant

Shrubs with a Purpose

Sometimes there can be an embarrassment of riches; I am sure that many a garden maker has so thought when confronted with the wealth of shrubs in a garden centre or in a nursery. Of course, there can never be too many, and the fear until quite recently was that there would be too few, with many fine plants for which there is a limited demand gradually disappearing from nurserymen's lists. But now we seem to be seeing far more choice plants being offered. Major private gardens open to the public also often have plant stalls at which less commonly seen plants can be obtained. My task now is to remind you of (or introduce you to) some of the shrubs which, collectively, will provide you with pleasure and interest around the year.

So let's start at the dawn of the new year and carry through to the following Christmas. I believe that many of us get enormous pleasure from our gardens in winter. What fun it is to potter around in the garden on a January morning, when the sun is shining and conifer colours sparkle and contrast with the filigree of branches provided by leafless trees, and to stop and marvel at the curiously contorted petals of the Chinese witch hazel, *Hamamelis mollis*, or the spread of colour from winter-flowering heaths, varieties of *Erica herbacea (carnea)*.

Indeed, the *herbacea* varieties make an admirable starting point, for the earliest of these to come into bloom, like the dwarf 'King George' with rosy-pink, brown-tipped blooms, are well into their flowering period by the time the new year comes. And January sees the flowering of that marvellous pair, 'Springwood White' and 'Springwood Pink', both of trailing habit and splendid ground coverers. Both have prominent brown anthers and, in the pure white 'Springwood White' in particular, this adds much to the attractions of the blooms. 'Springwood Pink' is a rose-pink colour. I'm particularly fond, too, of the low-growing 'Vivellii', which has carmine-red blooms (borne in February and March) with dark green foliage which turns to bronze in winter. A more recently introduced variety is 'Myretoun Ruby', which bears ruby-red flowers from February to April and has dark green foliage to provide a strong contrast. Another variety with much to contribute is 'Ann Sparkes', which has deep yellow foliage (tipped with dull red in winter) and purplish-red flowers from February to April. Taller than most at 12in. (30cm) (most fall within the 6 to 10in. [15–26cm] range) is 'Pink Spangles'. This has fine

25

deep pink flowers from January to March and covers the ground especially well.

The *Erica herbacea* varieties flower at a time of year when colour is especially welcome and are among the few heaths and heathers which will tolerate limy soils. If you have a neutral or acid soil, then you can take your pick from the enormous range of varieties of *Erica, Calluna* and *Daboecia* which will give colour throughout the year, with careful planning. These, mixed with a few choice conifers to provide contrast and height variations, can be an enormous pleasure. (See also the Wisley Handbook *Heaths and Heathers.*)

The winter-flowering heaths integrate splendidly with the Chinese witch hazel mentioned earlier, and the variety which I would suggest growing is *Hamamelis mollis* 'Pallida', a sulphur-yellow form which flowers especially freely, bearing its curious flowers with strap-like petals all along the bare branches. But note that all types of hamamelis must be given a neutral or acid soil, a sunny position (which they would obviously be given if planted near heaths), and a soil supplying a reasonable amount of moisture combined with good drainage. 'Pallida' will grow slowly to a height and spread of around 6ft (1.8m).

For February–March flowering one of the best-loved shrubs (of a size suitable for any garden) is the mezereon, *Daphne mezereum*, which produces its richly fragrant, purplish-red blooms thickly along the stems. It grows about 4ft (1.2m) tall and much the same wide, and its only fault is to occasionally decide that it has had enough and die off for no apparently good reason. For something so attractive the risk is worth taking. A well-drained soil is a necessity. *D. mezereum* is, of course, deciduous; an evergreen daphne which is of much the same size and decorative also at this time of year is *D. odora* 'Aureomarginata', this having pale green leaves margined with pale yellow and, in February and March, terminal heads of very fragrant, reddish-purple flowers. It is hardier than its slightly tender parent, *D. odora*, but it must be given a sheltered position.

One of the most valuable foliage shrubs for the garden in winter is *Elaeagnus pungens* 'Maculata', which quite slowly makes a bush up to 8ft (2.4m) tall and wide and which can, if necessary, be kept rather less than that by selective pruning. Its largish leaves are coloured a rich golden-yellow over a good part of their surface from the centre and bordered by dark green. Sometimes, branches will revert to pure green and these must be cut out. It has no special soil needs and will grow well on alkaline soils. Less well known is *E. pungens* 'Dicksonii', a slow-growing cultivar in which the yellow is carried in the outer part of the leaf rather than

Cytisus, broom, with its abundant pea-like flowers, prefers a well drained soil

the inner. The slow rate of growth could be an advantage.

For March–April flowering in the small garden I would strongly recommend *Magnolia stellata* and *Forsythia* 'Lynwood', the latter the best, I think, of its kind, with its rich yellow colouring, large flowers and the prodigality with which these are borne. Its dimensions are about 8ft by 8ft (2.4 × 2.4m). Forsythias are, of course, of the easiest cultivation, in sunshine or light shade. The star magnolia, *M. stellata*, is not a shrub for limy soils and it will do best on rather good loams which are moisture-retentive but well-drained. How delightful it is, though, with its shapely, rounded outline and spring burden of pure white flowers, each with many strap-shaped petals. It is much-branched and slow-growing but it can eventually make a bush some 10ft (3m) tall and wide.

If you have lime-free soil consider also some of the small rhododendrons like the 3ft (90cm) tall 'Tessa', which bears purplish pink, red-spotted flowers in March, and 'Seta', also March flowering, which has tubular pink flowers striped with a deeper shade of the same colour. This grows up to 5ft (1.5m) tall. As with all early-flowering rhododendrons, take care to keep them out of frost pockets or the blooms will be certain to suffer damage. Quite outstanding for April flowering is Elizabeth, which makes a spreading bush some 3 to 4ft (90cm–1.2m) tall, perfect for small gardens. Its very impressive trumpet-shaped blooms of bright scarlet are borne in trusses of up to five or six.

May sees the full flowering of the brooms, both *Genista* and *Cytisus* which share this common name. All need lashings of sunshine and light, well-drained soils in which to grow. A special favourite of mine is the dome-shaped Spanish gorse, *Genista hispanica*, a very prickly character indeed which literally smothers itself throughout May and early June with golden-yellow pea flowers. It grows about 3 to 4ft (90cm–1.2m) tall and more wide. If planted on a slight rise it looks marvellous with variously coloured sun roses (varieties of *Helianthemum nummularium*) around its base—in colours like orange, lemon-yellow, soft pink and bright yellow (even bright reds, if they are kept away from the bulk of the genista). A perfect choice for a bed on a retaining wall or for planting on a bank, where its arched branches can spill over, is the charming *Genista lydia*, which bears golden-yellow flowers from late May until late June. Only 2 to 3ft (60–90cm) tall, it has a spread of at least 6ft (1.8m).

Ideal for a raised bed is the procumbent *Cytisus kewensis*, no more than 1½ to 3ft (50–90cm) tall and with a spread of about 4 to 5ft (1.2–1.5m). This bears a mass of cream flowers in late April and May. I'm also very fond of the Warminster broom, *C. praecox*,

Elaeagnus pungens 'Maculata', planted mainly for its foliage, bears fragrant, creamy white flowers in mid to late autumn (see p.26)

larger at 5ft (1.5m) tall and wide, but very lovely indeed when smothered in cream flowers in May.

One of the most attractive variegated shrubs of medium size is undoubtedly *Weigela florida* 'Variegata', which bears pink foxglove-like flowers in May and June against a background of creamy white-edged leaves. The effect is cool and refreshing. It will usually make a bush 5 to 6ft (1.5–1.8m) tall and wide.

For flowering at the same time, another shrub not to be overlooked is the beautiful small Korean lilac named *Syringa velutina* (but still known to many as *S. palibiniana*), which does not usually grow over 5ft (1.5m) tall and wide and produces a wealth of small spikes of lilac-pink. Its leaves are small and roundish, of a fresh-looking light green. It should be given a home in a sunny position in well-drained soil.

The May- and June-flowering *Rhododendron yakushimanum* hybrids, so floriferous and attractive and compact of habit, are ideal for those small gardens where the soil is free of lime—and in gardens with alkaline soils they can, of course, be grown in containers, in lime-free compost. Naturally, there are variations in size and habit, but the average height of the considerable number now available is around 4ft (1.2m). Of special note are cultivars like the lavender 'Caroline Allbrook'; 'Percy Wiseman', with flowers of pink and cream which fade to creamy-white, with alluring effect; 'Dopey', a fine red; 'Hydon Hunter', with pink flowers rimmed at the petal edges with red and with orange spotting; and 'Morning Magic' in which pink buds open to blush-pink flowers which fade to white.

Two other genera which provide fine shrubs of modest size for early season flowering are *Escallonia* and *Philadelphus*. Of the escallonias—all of which grow well in any reasonable, well-drained soil, given a modicum of shelter—none is more calculated to please than 'Apple Blossom', which makes a bush some 4 to 5ft (1.2–1.5m) tall and wide and is in flower for months on end from early summer. As the name suggests, the blooms are a lovely shade of pink, merging to white low down on the petals. 'Glory of Donard', with carmine flowers, is another with a spread and height of about 5ft (1.5m).

The mock oranges (*Philadelphus*) have the great merit of doing well on thin, chalky soils as well as on any ordinary, well-drained soil. Sunshine or light shade is equally suitable. Varieties I would especially recommend include the creamy white, double-flowered 'Manteau d'Hermine', the white, single-flowered 'Avalanche', both up to 4ft (1.2m) tall and some 6ft (1.8m) wide, and 'Belle Etoile', another single with white, slightly maroon-blotched petals, which is several feet taller and wider.

Genista lydia, a superb dwarf shrub with a pendulous habit, may be kept more compact by light pruning immediately after flowering (see p. 28)

I'm very fond of *Senecio* 'Sunshine'. The spreading mound of grey foliage it provides is handsome in its own right, and it also makes an excellent foil for other plants of stronger colouring. In fact, the oval leaves are a soft green covered with a mass of grey hairs, as one sees when it is inspected close-to. Bright yellow daisy flowers are borne in quantity in late June and July, but it is as a foliage plant that it really excels itself. It requires a sunny position and a well-drained ordinary soil.

Euonymus fortunei 'Emerald an' Gold' is an excellent low-growing, foliage shrub. It is the colouring of the small, oval leaves which appeals so much: bright green and golden-yellow, with pinkish suffusions in the winter. It grows some 12 to 15in. (30–37cm) tall and the plants should be spaced about 12in. (30cm) apart to give thick cover. The variety 'Silver Queen' is of much the same height and has a spread of up to 3ft (90cm). Its

31

leaves are margined with silvery white and these can also take on pink suffusions in winter. Against a wall it will climb to a height of 5 to 6ft (1.5–1.8m) and have a similar spread. These are suitable for sunny or lightly shaded positions.

The carpeting *Hebe pinguifolia* 'Pagei', with its dainty, glaucous bluish-grey leaves, is another useful plant. I grow it with the long-flowering *Geranium sanguineum lancastriense* 'Splendens', which has rose-pink flowers (the hebe is about 9in. [22cm] tall, the geranium 12in. [30cm]), for they complement each other very well. They should, of course, be planted in a sunny position.

I am very taken with the effectiveness of the compact-growing form of the deciduous *Physocarpus opulifolius* named 'Dart's Gold' as a summer-long foliage shrub of small size. A wealth of three- or five-lobed leaves, which start the season golden-yellow and only very slowly take on light green suffusions, are borne on a well-rounded bush some 2½ft (75cm) tall. White flowers are carried in June but these add little to its decorative value. Given the right companions in a mixed border, it can be extremely eye-catching. Its hardiness is not in doubt for it came through temperatures as low as 3°F (– 16°C) in my garden in January 1986—with no adverse affect. It is happiest in moist but well-drained soil and needs exposure to sunshine to bring out the colour of the leaves.

On the face of it it sounds incongruous that a fine house plant should double-up as an excellent garden shrub of large proportions, but that is exactly what *Fatsia japonica* does—at least in warmer parts of the country, in reasonably sheltered positions. It can make a bush of spreading habit some 15ft (4.5m) tall and wide but it would be much more usual for it to settle down at about half that size. The palmate leaves—often as much as 15 or 16in. (37–40cm) across—have up to nine lobes, a leathery texture and rich green colouring. It has very pronounced architectural merit. It is not at all surprising that it should also make a fine subject for a large container, but one thing which must be watched, if it is grown in that way, is its welfare in arctic weather conditions. The root system is more vulnerable and when such conditions threaten take the precaution of wrapping sacking or other protective material around the container.

Small gardens can often provide sunny, sheltered corners and that is just the kind of spot for the Jerusalem sage, *Phlomis fruticosa*, an evergreen with grey-green leaves up to 5in. (12cm) long of sage-like appearance and distinctive bright yellow, stalk-less and hooded flowers which are borne in whorls during the first half of summer. It has a rather sprawly habit and associates particularly well with paving, over which it can be allowed to extend. It grows to about 3 to 4ft (90cm–1.2m) tall and 5 to 6ft

The deeply lobed, glossy leaves of *Fatsia japonica* provide interesting shape and texture in a small garden

(1.5–1.8m) wide. Its growth is rather soft, however, and it is liable to get cut back in winter.

For the length of their flowering (usually the summer through) and the ease of their cultivation, given a well-drained position, there is every reason to find space for potentillas, especially garden-raised hybrids like 'Primrose Beauty', pale primrose yellow in colour and some 4ft (1.2m) tall and 5ft (1.5m) wide: 'Klondyke', deep yellow, and a little smaller; and the rich yellow 'Elizabeth', which is lower-growing still and exceptionally long flowering. This is about 3ft (90cm) tall and up to 7 or 8ft (2.1–2.4m) wide. 'Red Ace' is the vermilion-red variety which caused such a stir some years ago by introducing a new colour to this flower. It can live up to its name but it can also be disappointing, for in wet weather and in very hot, dry weather the rich colour fades. The delightful 'Princess' has soft pink flowers which also tend to fade in hot, very dry spells. It grows some 2½ft (75cm) tall and wide.

No shrub of medium size is more deserving of a sunny place in the garden than the fine *Hypericum* 'Hidcote', which produces a profusion of large, saucer-shaped golden yellow flowers on a domed bush some 4ft (1.2m) high and 6ft (1.8m) wide from July into the autumn. It will do well in any reasonable, well-drained soil. From July also until September a bush of a lacecap hydrangea could be much appreciated for its attractive flowerheads—say the lovely *H. macrophylla* 'Bluewave' or 'Mariesii', both rose-pink or blue, depending on the soil type, or 'Whitewave' with pinkish centres and white, outer fertile flowers. These hydrangeas, like the ball-headed varieties, have their colouring determined by the pH of the soil, and thus on alkaline soils varieties which are normally blue become pink or red.

The hortensias appear later under plants for containers (see p. 229). Brief mention, however, of a variety of *H. serrata* which has blooms of globular shape, just like those of the hortensias but a little smaller. This is 'Preziosa' and its garden value is considerable, for these blooms are salmon-pink in colour, turning to a deeper shade as the season advances. With those go purple-tinged young foliage and stems. Its height is around 4 to 4½ft (1.3m) and it can be grown in sunshine or light shade, like all the hydrangeas. What must be avoided at all costs is subjecting them to dryness at the roots, especially in the growing season.

For late July and August flowering there is *Hydrangea paniculata* 'Grandiflora', which produces cone-shaped panicles of creamy-white flowers up to 18in. (45cm) long. These become suffused with pink as they age. It can grow into a large bush with arched branches having a height of 10ft (3m) or more, but it can be kept much smaller by hard pruning in early spring, just before

The saucer-like flowers of *Potentilla* 'Elizabeth' give good value, appearing from late spring to early autumn

growth gets under way. This will result in fewer but larger flowers. It needs a good rich loam.

A delightful small shrub for September flowering is *Caryopteris* × *clandonensis* 'Arthur Simmonds' which produces tufty blue flowers on a grey-green-leaved bush some 3 to 4ft (90cm–1.2m) tall and wide. It will succeed in any well-drained soil in a sunny position but is liable to be cut back severely in hard winters. For this reason it is often necessary to hard prune it at the start of spring, which in any case leads to better flowers.

The useful and easily pleased cotoneasters are at their best in the autumn. If you have a bank to cover there is nothing better for the purpose than the prostrate evergreen *C. dammeri*, which has a spread of as much as 9 or 10ft (2.7–3m) and smothers itself with brilliant red fruits in autumn. Another evergreen for the same purpose is *C. conspicuus* 'Decorus', which has a height of up to 3ft (90cm) and a spread of as much as 10ft (3m). They should preferably be given a sunny position, to ensure free-fruiting.

November is most definitely the month of *Mahonia* 'Charity', that superb evergreen shrub which opens its terminal racemes of rich yellow, fragrant flowers—borne up to 20 to a cluster and arching over in foot-long trails—against a background of truly spectacular leaves, each one of which is comprised of up to 21 spiny leaflets of dark green. It makes a large shrub, at least 8ft (2.4m) tall and 6ft (1.8m) wide (sometimes quite a lot more, but it can be pruned with care in spring). It grows well in any soil well supplied with moisture and well-drained, in sunshine or light shade. Flowering continues until late January.

For December I think it must be that old favourite, the evergreen laurustinus, *Viburnum tinus*, so valuable for its winter flowers, or rather its more compact form, 'Eve Price', which makes an attractive bush of 7 to 8ft (2–2.4m) tall and wide with smaller leaves than the parent plant, densely borne, and red buds which open to white, pink-tinged flowers. Against the dark green foliage, these flowers are a very handsome sight, and bloom throughout the winter. The excellent variety 'Gwenllian' makes a rather larger bush than 'Eve Price' and is usually free in producing blue berries which blend beautifully with the flowers.

Lastly, just a word about that other evergreen *Viburnum* species, *V. davidii*, which is attractive all the year round as low ground cover—it has a height of about 2ft (60cm) a spread of about 3ft (90cm)—with its narrowly oval, very dark green leaves, glossy and deeply veined, and (at times anyway) turquoise blue fruits if male specimens are planted with the female.

Making the Most of Roses

Roses deserve, and indeed were given early on, a handbook to themselves in this series, so my comments are restricted to brief mention of varieties which I believe have considerable potential in small gardens. Obviously, all the compact floribunda varieties are ideal, while climbing roses of all kinds must have a special role to play. Likewise the best of the modern bush roses (the large-flowered and cluster-flowered cultivars which we used to know as hybrid teas and floribundas), if their special qualities give them an edge over other contenders for valuable space. Shrub roses of the repeat-flowering kind? A few, where they, too, can make a real contribution; but not, alas, those old garden roses with one, all-too-brief, season of colour. And what about the miniatures, now gaining so much in popularity? These certainly do have a place in the small garden, especially for raised beds and for display near the home where their small stature can be an asset.

Clearly, the shorter cluster-flowered roses have an important part in the small garden; varieties, for instance, like the bright orange-scarlet 'Topsi' and creamy-white 'Bianco', which are only 1¼ft (38cm) tall, and excellent performers like the canary-yellow 'Kim', apricot-pink 'Peek-a-Boo' and light pink, white-eyed 'Regensberg', which are no more than 1½ft (45cm) tall. A little taller again, nearer 2ft (60cm), are the scarlet 'Trumpeter' and the yellow 'Bright Smile'. There are so many varieties in a wide colour range from which to make a choice.

A 3ft (90cm) tall cluster-flowered rose which looks delightful in association with paving is 'Yesterday', this carrying its small flowers in sprays which start off pink and fade to a lavender shade as they age—a charming combination. The foliage is small and thus in scale. The other rose which never looks better than in this kind of setting is 'Ballerina', a shrub rose with hybrid musk blood which makes a mass of growths to a height of 3 to 4ft (90cm–1.2m), is rather sprawly and delights the summer through with clusters of pale pink, white-eyed single blooms set among pale green foliage. 'Marjorie Fair' is a recent offspring from it, this having deep red flowers with a white eye. That old stager 'The Fairy' is another lovely variety, with soft peach, rosette-forming blooms carried over a very long period and attractive, glossy foliage. It grows some 3ft (90cm) tall and has a spreading habit.

Could there be a better large-flowered rose for a set-piece planting than 'Silver Jubilee'? With its beautiful, full blooms of pink, peach and cream and its good foliage, this is sure to be with us for many a year. Others of real distinction among the quite recently introduced cultivars are the deep yellow 'Freedom' and the highly fragrant, salmon-pink 'Paul Shirville', as well as the primrose-coloured 'Peaudouce'.

Of the numerous large-flowered climbers for growing on pillars—so suitable for giving height in the small garden while taking up little space—my choice would be 'Handel', a first-class variety with cream blooms flushed at the edges of the petals with rose-pink; multi-coloured 'Joseph's Coat', an amalgam of yellow, red and orange; 'Parkdirektor Riggers', brilliant scarlet; 'Pink Perpétue', clear pink with a carmine-pink reverse; and 'Compassion', a salmon-pink variety.

For the house walls, without question, it would be first of all the exquisite 'Climbing Cécile Brunner' and 'Phyllis Bide'. 'Climbing Cécile Brunner' is a glorious sight in early summer when smothering a large section of wall with its small, exquisitely shapely blooms of blush pink, and more flowers arrive during the rest of the summer although not in the quantities produced during the first flush. 'Phyllis Bide' usually grows to a height of about 7 or 8ft (2.1–2.4m) although it can go considerably higher, and this produces, against a. background of very attractive foliage, a succession of small, full-petalled, salmon-shaded, yellow flowers from early summer until deep into autumn. This much-neglected rose (raised in 1923) is deserving of far wider attention.

What a pity it is that that most beautiful of roses 'Mme Grégoire Staechelin' has such a relatively brief season of flowering, for its highly fragrant, large blooms, coral-pink shaded scarlet, make it one of the most desirable of all roses to have in the garden in June and July. This strong-growing, large-flowered climber, so stunning against a light coloured stone wall (it will do well with a north or east aspect) is still well worth giving space. Beauty and repeat-flowering go together in the splendid 'Mermaid', the *bracteata* climber which will climb to a height of 25ft (9m) or more and delight with its large, single blooms of pale yellow set off by a boss of amber stamens. This is a variety for a south- or west-facing wall, and not a rose for cold gardens.

Going back to the shrub roses, two that I would certainly want to fit in if at all possible would be, first, 'Golden Wings', a highly attractive fragrant variety of modest height (only 4ft [1.2m]) which bears large, single, pale yellow flowers with amber stamens throughout the summer. Then the much taller 'Fred Loads' with its brilliant vermilion-orange, single blooms. This grows to a height of 6 or 7ft (1.8–2.1m) and could give a real lift to a sunny corner of the garden.

The exquisite 'Phyllis Bide' (left), a fine rose for training against a wall, and 'Mme Grégoire Staechlin' (right), whose blooms are followed by large hips if not dead-headed

As to the miniatures, more and more of these seem to come along each year now, to join such excellent varieties as orange-red 'Starina'; red, striped white 'Stars 'n' Stripes'; pink 'Sweet Fairy'; and yellow and pink 'Baby Masquerade'. Newer cultivars include 'Dresden Doll', the pink miniature moss rose; yellow 'Rise 'n' Shine'; orange 'Hula Girl'; and coral-red 'Fashion Flame'. Raised beds, as I remarked earlier, and containers, are the natural homes for these.

Shade-loving *Hosta undulata* 'Albomarginata' has superb foliage which, unfortunately, is enticing to slugs

Perennials for Pleasure

Everyone who gardens for enjoyment knows the unending possibilities it offers as a leisure pursuit. What is not so often realised—for there is no reason why it should be given conscious thought—is the remarkable ability of gardening to evolve, with the passage of time; to stay in tune with changing life styles. The herbaceous perennials provide a perfect example of this, for, half a century ago, they were associated in the mind's eye with spacious, formal, herbaceous borders and with the organised confusion (if I may put it that way) of the cottage garden—with little in between. Now, in a word, they have been 'liberated', first through the development of the mixed border—of which there are such fine examples at Wisley—and then through the island-bed concept. It was Alan Bloom, the perennial plant specialist, who opened my eyes—as well as those of countless others—to the possibilities of this very large and fascinating group of plants.

Clearly, in the space at my disposal, I can only mention a limited number of these plants; but I have chosen them with care as being among the best, at least in my opinion, if the aim is to make maximum use of limited space. Two factors are of over-riding importance when choosing perennials for the small garden: the quality of the plant (obviously) and the length of time during which it is likely to make a contribution to the garden. That doesn't mean that plants with rather short periods of display should be ruled out, but priority should be given to those which show up well in this respect.

Let us start with the hostas, which personify for me all that is best in perennials—a wide spread of interest, real quality and a large measure of adaptability, for although they are at their happiest in light shade, they are perfectly satisfactory in sunny positions provided they are well supplied with root moisture. But do concentrate on planting the most elegant of the species, varieties and hybrids. My favourite, without question, is one that grows to about 2ft (60cm), namely *H. crispula*—a joy from spring to autumn with its long, wavy-margined, sharp-pointed leaves of dark green, edged with white. Running a close second, however, is *H. undulata*, with pronounced undulation of the leaves as the name suggests, and a bold white sector irregularly margined with bright green. Both species bear lilac-coloured flowers in July and are roughly the same height. Outstanding also are the 2½ft (75cm) *H. fortunei* 'Albopicta', with leaves which start the season mainly rich yellow edged with green and which gradually change to primrose-yellow and green and then two shades of light and dark green; 'Thomas Hogg' in which the handsome leaves are broadly margined with cream; and 'Royal Standard' which carries its pure white flowers from August well into autumn above bold, fresh-green, heart-shaped leaves. The other two both have lilac-coloured blooms, those of 'Albopicta' arriving in mid-summer and those of 'Thomas Hogg' in early summer.

Two others I would mention are H. *lancifolia* and H. *tardiflora*. In both cases the name reflects the character of the plant. *Hosta lancifolia* has shiny, deep green, lance-shaped leaves and bears lilac flowers from July to September on 2ft (60cm) stems. *Hosta tardiflora* is only half that height, has shiny dark green leaves and bears lilac-mauve flowers in September and October. All hostas appreciate a good soil, with its ability to retain moisture while still remaining well-drained. This facility can be improved, of course, if necessary, by working in peat, garden compost, composted bark fibre or the like before planting, and mulching thereafter in spring with the same kind of materials.

If you believe, as I do, that yellow is a colour of which it is difficult to have too much in the garden, then allow me to suggest three quite different kinds of perennials which will provide this colour over a long period. First, a doronicum with its daisy-like blooms, the German-raised 'Spring Beauty' ('Frühlingspracht'), which produces a mass of showy, double flowers of rich yellow between late March and the end of May. As it has a height of only 1½ft (45cm) there are many spots in which this can be used, especially as it will do well in any reasonable soil in sunshine or light shade.

Next, that very reliable and free-flowering coreopsis, C. *verticillata* 'Grandiflora', also 1½ft (45cm) tall, which bears its golden-yellow daisy flowers above very thin, fern-like foliage from the beginning of July to the end of September. This must be exposed to plenty of sunshine. Then, to round off the season, the splendid cone-flower or black-eyed Susan, the 2½ft (75cm) tall *Rudbeckia fulgida* 'Goldsturm', another sun-lover, which associates beautifully with *Sedum* 'Autumn Joy' and S. *spectabile* varieties like 'Brilliant'. The overlap of flowering times occurs in September and October and the sedum would be planted in front with its height of about 1½ft (45cm). 'Goldsturm', with its bright yellow flowers so splendidly set off by the black central cones, is in flower from early July until September and often deep into October.

There is no perennial which gives better value for the space occupied than *Salvia nemorosa* 'Superba'. A bold clump of this 3ft

(90cm) tall plant is a fine sight. It throws up a thick mass of bluish-purple flower spikes in the July–September period and associates beautifully with numerous yellow-flowered plants, preferably with contrasting flower shapes. The similarly sized, flat-headed *Achillea* 'Coronation Gold' springs readily to mind, both having the same need for plenty of sunshine. Any reasonably good soil will suffice.

The herbaceous geraniums are first-rate garden plants. Consider *Geranium* 'Johnson's Blue', for example. This splendid plant produces a succession of light blue flowers on $1\frac{1}{2}$ft (45cm) stems from May right through to September and has handsome, deeply cut foliage. Now *G. psilostemon* cannot match 'Johnson's Blue' for length of flowering, but it can for sheer beauty. Its deeply cut leaves are large and of mid-green colouring and it makes a bushy mound some 3ft (90cm) tall which forms a backdrop, in June and July, for the lovely magenta-crimson, black-centred flowers. In a word, it is superb.

Both of those just mentioned are excellent ground cover plants, like so many of their kind, in light shade or in sunny positions. I will confine my remarks to just two more, 'Claridge Druce' and *G. endressii* 'A. T. Johnson'. The first is a hybrid of real worth which makes thick clumps of deeply cut leaves and, in June and July, bears lilac-pink flowers. It is a first-class, $1\frac{1}{2}$ft (45cm) tall ground-cover plant for sunshine or shade. *G. endressii* 'A. T. Johnson' is 1ft (30cm) tall, bears silvery pink flowers from June to September, and is also an admirable ground-cover plant.

Another genus which gives good value for the owner of a small garden is euphorbia, with the benefits coming in the spring and early summer months. The shade-tolerant and very showy *Euphorbia robbiae* is a good plant to have in the garden for it provides excellent ground cover, making a dense mat some $1\frac{1}{2}$ft (45cm) tall with its rosettes of dark green leaves topped in May and June by yellow bracts. *Euphorbia griffithii* 'Fireglow' is another very useful plant, although taller ($2\frac{1}{2}$ft [75cm]) and at its decorative best in early summer, when it produces its orange-red flowers. This is better in sunshine but is perfectly satisfactory in shade. Likewise the $1\frac{1}{2}$ft (45cm) tall *E. polychroma* (which used to be known as *E. epithymoides*), which is very distinctive in April and May with its bright yellowish green flowers. Again, they are good ground coverers.

Do try and find room, if you can, for *E. characias*, for this is a superb specimen plant some 4ft (1.2m) tall and wide which produces a mass of green, brown-centred blooms in large terminal heads in May and June. You can grow this in sunshine or light shade. None of these euphorbias has any soil fads.

The oriental poppies (varieties of *Papaver orientale*) tend to die down quite early in the summer and so, if you are not careful, leave ugly holes in the planting scheme of which they are part. But that problem can be easily overcome by siting them behind leafy, low-growing perennials. Their flowers are a joy as spring gives way to summer, whether they are those of orange-scarlet 'Marcus Perry'; 'Perry's White', white, with near black blotches; or maybe the delicately coloured salmon-pink 'Mrs Perry', which is the one I like best of all. In recent years, too, a spate of excellent new varieties has arrived, among them 'Picotee', salmon on a white ground and with frilly-edged petals; 'Harvest Moon', orange; and 'Black and White', white with black markings at the base of the petals. All are between $2\frac{1}{2}$ and 3ft (70–90cm) tall and will grow in any ordinary, well-drained soil in a sunny position.

That brings me to the June-flowering herbaceous peonies— truly magnificent plants, which, quite apart from their flowers, contribute with their foliage to the appearance of the garden. It is often overlooked that the foliage colours most attractively in autumn, to soft browns, ochres and yellows. But, of course, it is the flowers which really matter. If I were to pick out a few of the

Paeonia 'Festiva Maxima' has large heavy blooms which may need staking (see p. 45)

double-flowered *Paeonia lactiflora* varieties, they would be deep rose-red 'Felix Crousse'; white, flecked reddish-purple 'Festiva Maxima'; apple-blossom pink 'Sarah Bernhardt'. Of the so-called Imperial varieties (single varieties with centres of petal-like staminodes), it would be the superb pink and creamy yellow 'Bowl of Beauty', 3ft (90cm) tall and a glorious sight in early summer. These will do well in sunshine or light shade in a nicely moist soil, but the more sunshine the better the flowering. If you want to grow something in the connoisseur class, however, it must be *P. mlokosewitschii*, a Caucasian species some 2½ft (70cm) tall which produces glorious cup-shaped blooms of pale yellow with a prominent centrepiece of golden yellow stamens in April against a background of pale green foliage.

I find the goat's beard, *Aruncus dioicus* (*A. sylvester*), an invaluable plant in early summer when it produces those marvellous plumes of creamy white flowers on stems 4 to 5ft (1.2–1.5m) tall. I grow it with cream-coloured shrub roses and mauve rhododendrons which also flower in June, but it is equally desirable with many other companions. It is best in the kind of light shade provided by a nearby canopy of high-branched trees. Again, plenty of soil moisture is desirable. If height is a problem there is a smaller version of it—the 2½ft (75cm) tall *A. dioicus* 'Kneiffii', which has similarly coloured flower plumes. Both have ferny-looking foliage which is an attraction until the end of the season.

The day lilies (or *Hemerocallis*) are popular for two very good reasons: they are easy to grow and, depending on variety, will provide a succession of colour with their lily-like flowers from early summer until September. That is not all, however, for the clumps of arched, grass-like leaves start the season a pale green which can be very attractive in spring, with this colour deepening as the weeks pass to a strong green. In autumn the leaves turn to yellow in their dying days. Orange, reds, pinks and yellows are the flower colours available, and new varieties of merit are coming along all the time. Established varieties to look out for especially are the small-flowered 'Golden Chimes', a fine deep yellow; rich crimson 'Stafford'; and primrose-coloured 'Whichford', with greenish centres to the flowers. Mostly these are 2½ to 3ft (70–90cm) tall, but some fall outside this range and notably the new 'Stella d' Oro', with orange-throated, canary yellow flowers, which is only 1¾ft (53cm) tall.

Don't rule out the tall bearded irises even though they provide only a few weeks of colour in May–June. Just a few carefully chosen varieties can be well worth while, if one allows that the sword-like foliage makes a splendid foil for other plants of different habit. These, of course, need plenty of sunshine and well-drained soil—don't make the mistake of planting the rhizomes too deeply; these should have their tops level with the soil surface. Excellent varieties include the pale blue 'Jane Phillips', yellow and chestnut red 'Staten Island' and 'Berkeley Gold', golden yellow.

The iris tribe generally is fascinating, but the only other ones which I shall mention here are the variegated forms of *I. pallida* and *I. foetidissima*. The first, for planting in a sunny position in well-drained soil, is available in two forms, one having white longitudinal stripes on the grey-green, sword-like leaves, the other yellow stripes. Of the two I find the white the more compelling in the garden, but both are excellent plants some 2 to 3ft (60–90cm) tall which can have a dramatic impact if several are planted together. These bear lavender-coloured flowers which are of less importance than the foliage.

The Gladwyn iris, *I. foetidissima*, is, of course, a good plant for shade and is very handsome indeed when the seed pods split open revealing the scarlet seeds. Its form 'Variegata' has cream longitudinal leaf variegation and is another desirable plant to help bring character to a mixed planting.

While on the subject of variegation, don't overlook the charms of the low-growing ground-coverer named *Brunnera macrophylla* 'Variegata' which has heart-shaped leaves heavily marked with cream and, in April, bright blue, forget-me-not-like flowers borne in tiny sprays. It is a good plant for light shade and nicely moist soil—soil and conditions which well suit the pulmonarias or lung-worts (which also have very interesting, mottled foliage). One of the best is the foot-high (30cm) *Pulmonaria saccharata* 'Pink Dawn', which flowers from March to May and has funnel-shaped blooms of rose-pink complemented most attractively by the white-mottled foliage.

Similar conditions to the above would be just right also for the willow gentian, *Gentiana asclepiadea*, a delight between July and September when it bears, on arched 2½ft (75cm) long stems, rich blue, narrowly funnel-shaped flowers against a background of willow-like leaves. It is a lovely plant and there is a fine variety named 'Knightshayes' which has flowers of deeper colour than the parent.

What cheerfulness the crocosmias bring to the garden in the second half of summer, especially the species *Crocosmia masonorum* and its outstanding form 'Firebird'. These carry from late July to September arching sprays of orange flowers above the sword-like foliage, which is typical of crocosmias generally and makes such an effective foil for the blooms. Its height is about 2½ft

Yellow kniphofias are prominent in this large-scale herbaceous border

(75cm). Somewhat taller (a little over 3ft [90cm]) is the hybrid 'Lucifer', with *Curtonus paniculatus* on one side of its parentage and crocosmia on the other (these genera are closely related). This comparative newcomer is a superb plant with arching sprays of brilliant red flowers borne in July and August, or from late June in some gardens. It has good foliage and has proved to be a very strong-growing plant. In flower, it makes a great impact. The flowers are also excellent for cutting for the home.

Culturally, the crocosmias are easy plants to please, growing well in any soil of average quality which is well drained but nicely retentive of moisture. They grow from corms and should rightly be placed with the bulbous plants in this book, but among the perennials they find their natural home. They are best grown in sunny, sheltered positions. They are clump-forming and spread quickly and lifting and division is usually necessary every third or fourth year to maintain quality. This is best done in early spring but can be done in early autumn.

Space runs short but there are a few other plants which simply must be included. *Polygonum bistorta* 'Superbum', for instance, $2\frac{1}{2}$ to 3ft (75–90cm) tall and a wonderful sight when its pink poker-like blooms are borne above the tumbling mass of rather coarse leaves between May and July. It will grow well in sunshine or light shade and in a sunny position is ideal for mixing with the lighter-coloured brooms—those with cream flowers like *Cytisus praecox*. It must have an adequate supply of root moisture, but otherwise its needs are few. Another plant which always attracts attention when it is in bloom is *Stachys macrantha* 'Superba'. It makes a ground-covering mat of dark green leaves with attractively wrinkled surfaces above which are borne in June and July whorls of rosy-mauve, hooded flowers on $1\frac{1}{2}$ to 2ft (45–60cm) stems. It flowers best in a sunny position but is satisfactory, too, in light shade.

Then there is that outstanding aster, *A. × frikartii*, which bears a mass of lavender blue, daisy-like flowers with orange centres from July to September—this makes a marvellous companion for *Rudbeckia fulgida* 'Goldsturm' which I mentioned earlier (see p. 42). And, of course, in a different category again, the perennial adored by all flower arranging ladies: *Alchemilla mollis*, the lady's mantle, with its roundish, scalloped, pale green leaves and dainty sprays of greenish yellow flowers throughout most of the summer. It will grow equally well in sunshine or shade.

Getting towards the end of the year, you should be aware of the value of *Schizostylis coccinea* (preferably in its form 'Major'), which bears racemes of bright red star-shaped flowers above sword-like leaves from late September to November. There are two excellent pink-flowered varieties, 'Viscountess Byng' and 'Mrs Hegarty'. In all but favoured gardens they must be given a sunny, sheltered position in a wall bed, and they must be grown in soil which retains plenty of moisture in the growing season. The rhizomes should be protected in winter by giving them a covering of dry litter.

A plant which is little known and very useful for late colour—and as a useful ground cover—is *Liriope muscari*. This has grassy, evergreen leaves of dark green and produces from August to November spikes of grape-hyacinth-like blooms of violet-purple on stems 1ft (30cm) tall. You can grow it in any ordinary soil in sunshine or light shade.

By the end of the year we can enjoy the beautiful flowers of the Algerian iris, *Iris unguicularis* (still often known as *I. stylosa*). These flowers may be anything from pale lavender-blue to something approaching purple in colour. It must be given a home in full sun (so that the rhizomes will get thoroughly baked in summer), sheltered from the elements and in a poorish but impeccably well-drained soil.

The hellebores are invaluable, from the Christmas rose, *Helleborus niger*, which again needs a nicely sheltered home, preferably in a bed against a north-facing wall if this is not exposed to cold winds (for this plant must not be allowed to dry out in hot sunshine in summer) to the Lenten roses (varieties of *H. orientalis*). Then there is the pale-green-flowered stinking hellebore, *H. foetidus*, with its handsome much segmented foliage; and, the finest of them all, the Corsican hellebore, *H. corsicus*, with its large heads of cup-shaped, pale green flowers and very handsome leaves.

Some gardeners take a rather superior attitude towards the bergenias, describing the leaves, for instance, as 'cabbagey'. They are first-rate plants, make magnificent ground cover with their evergreen foliage and are very pleasing in flower with the various species, varieties and hybrids providing welcome colour from March (or even earlier) to May. My favourites are the 1 to 1½ft (30–45cm) tall 'Ballawley' with rose-red flowers in March and April and leaves which become suffused with bronzy-red in winter; pure white 'Silberlicht' ('Silver Light'), 1ft (30cm) tall and April–May flowering; and *B.* x *schmidtii* which has especially attractive, bright green leaves and pale pink flowers from the beginning of March or even earlier until April. *Bergenia cordifolia* 'Purpurea' is the variety most frequently encountered, this having rounded leaves (which take on purplish overtones in winter) and purplish pink flowers in bold heads in March and April. It is an excellent plant.

Genista hispanica (see p.28), Spanish broom, with dense clusters of golden yellow flowers, contrasting with the taller shape of *Euphorbia characias wulfenii*

A soothing mix of foliage, including ferns and irises which appreciate a cool, moist setting

Raised Beds

Raised beds have really come into their own in recent years as an aid to the handicapped and the elderly. But such beds have an application in a great many gardens purely as a design feature which will allow small plants, from alpines and rock plants generally to small bulbous flowers and even shrubs and perennials tending towards the miniature, to be displayed to maximum advantage.

Such a feature will, in the nature of things, have impeccable drainage, and that is something so many plants enjoy. The bulbous flowers I have mentioned, the smallest of slow-growing conifers, miniature roses and miniature shrubs like the creeping willow, *Salix uva-ursi*, or the golden-yellow stemmed *Hebe armstrongii*, which has closely adpressed leaves of yellowish green (now correctly known as *H. ochracea*), are all suitable candidates.

Raised beds come in for full consideration in Joe Elliott's *Alpines the Easy Way* in this series. If you are interested in having such a feature without specialising then I would suggest a visit to Wisley to see the beds there.

A raised bed planted with tulips, wallflowers and forget-me-nots

Colour from Annuals and Biennials

Hardy annuals first, because minimal facilities are needed to grow these to perfection. Perhaps two of the most significant hardy annuals to be introduced in recent years are the mallows, *Lavatera* 'Silver Cup' and 'Mont Blanc'. These are very impressive plants indeed, making bushy specimens which literally smother themselves with bold trumpet flowers from July to September from seeds sown direct in the border in spring. To obtain plants which will come into flower earlier, seeds can be sown under glass in March with the resulting plants being set out in May. 'Silver Cup' is rose-pink in colour, with streaks of deeper pink on the petals, and $2\frac{1}{2}$ft (75cm) tall; 'Mont Blanc', as the name suggests, is dazzling white and grows to 2ft (60cm) tall.

Sweet peas are almost everybody's favourite, and it would be difficult to overestimate the importance of developments like the splendid Jet Set Mixed strain, which provides such fine-quality flowers on plants only 3ft (90cm) tall. For the small garden particularly they are a delight, both for garden display (perhaps grown as a low hedge between two parts of the garden) and for cutting. Likewise, the slightly smaller Little Elfin Mixed strain. Then there is the Patio strain which is only 1ft (30cm) tall. This is ideal for confined quarters, and for growing in containers.

Nasturtiums are, of course, invaluable for providing bright colour, and of these the dwarf Jewel strain with its excellent colour range is ideal for growing in containers. For this last use, too, keep *Convolvulus* 'Blue Flash' in mind. This is a striking plant with its mass of rich blue, white and yellow-centred blooms.

The lovely little Californian poppies, or eschscholzias, are easy to grow well in sunny positions (like the nasturtiums and convolvulus just mentioned). Good mixtures include Monarch Art shades and the very pretty Ballerina mixture in which the flower petals are fluted. All come in a good range of colours.

Then there are the godetias of which the best, I think most of us would agree, is the exquisite 'Sybil Sherwood', 15in. (38cm) tall. It belongs to the azalea-flowered section and bears salmon-pink blooms edged with white, in abundance, over a very long period in summer. A perfect companion for it is the straw-coloured 1 to $1\frac{1}{2}$ft (30–45cm) tall squirrel-tail grass, *Hordeum jubatum*, also annual and available from some seed firms. And while on the subject of grasses, don't overlook the charms of the pearl grass, *Briza maxima* (often called quaking grass, which is a

Rudbeckias, or coneflowers, enjoy the sun and well-drained soil. The flower-heads are excellent for cutting

name applied to the brizas generally); this grows about 15in. (38cm) tall and is a very elegant sight indeed with its mass of pendent spikelets nodding in the slightest breeze.

One of the loveliest annuals, in my opinion, is *Limnanthes douglasii*, a Californian native, which was long ago dubbed the poached egg flower here (from the appearance of the white, yellow-centred flowers). Give it a sunny position and it is very easily pleased. Cornflowers (*Centaurea cyanus* varieties), annual poppies (forms of *Papaver rhoeas*, like the Shirley Single Mixed strain) and love-in-the-mist (*Nigella damascena* varieties like 'Miss Jekyll' and the Persian Jewels strain) can all give a great deal of pleasure.

The half-hardy kind, of course, are a little more trouble to raise for they cannot be planted out until late May or early June, after proper hardening-off. Of these, the most significant in my reckoning are the forms of *Begonia semperflorens*; the petunias; forms of *Phlox drummondii*; the rudbeckias 'Marmalade', and 'Rustic Dwarfs' and the double and semi-double flowered 'Goldilocks'; tobacco plants (*Nicotiana*); marigolds (*Tagetes*) of various kinds; and dahlias like the single-flowered Dandy strain and the semi-double 'Redskin'.

The fibrous-rooted *Begonia semperflorens* varieties and strains are available in almost bewildering quantity. My favourites are the compact-growing Organdy mixture of some 8in. (20cm) in height, an excellent range of colours from red and pink to white and green and bronze-foliaged plants, and the taller (1ft [30cm]) 'Danica Red' and 'Danica Rose'. These begonias and others of their kind continue flowering well into the autumn and if you lift some plants then, pot them up and bring them indoors when they will continue to produce blooms deep into winter. Marvellous value! So too are the Nonstop strain of tuberous-rooted begonia. The colour range is excellent, the flowers are double and the name Nonstop is an accurate portrayal of their garden performance. These can be grown from seed, which is why they are mentioned here, or tubers can be purchased.

Of the petunias the Resisto strain does, as claimed, stand up especially well to bad weather. Again, these come in a delightful range of colours and in dwarf versions a few inches shorter than the rest at 1ft (30cm) tall. Turning to *Phlox drummondii*, my choice would be Beauty Mixed, 15in. (38cm) tall and with large flowers in a good range of colours, and the Carnival mixture which is slightly shorter.

Rudbeckia 'Marmalade' and 'Rustic Dwarfs' are superb garden plants, and excellent for cutting into the bargain. 'Marmalade' has golden-yellow ray flowers with bold black discs; 'Rustic Dwarfs', again with black discs, is a mixture of bronze, mahogany-red and yellow. The double and semi-double flowered 'Goldilocks' is the most recent to be introduced, the colour golden yellow. All are around 2ft (60cm) tall. Although they are very much plants for sunny positions, they stand up remarkably well to adverse weather, especially the first two. These can be given the usual half-hardy treatment (sowing in heat between February and April) or can be treated as biennials.

Earlier on I mentioned the nicotianas, or tobacco plants. A delightful strain to use to fill pockets in a mixed planting is the 2 to 2½ft (60–75cm) tall Sensation Mixed, with flowers which keep open all through the day. The same applies to the 1ft (30cm) tall Nicki Mixed, an F₁ strain with an excellent colour range. The fragrance of the Nicki mixture is especially strong, this coming out fully, as with the tobacco plants generally, in the evening.

The range of marigolds, or *Tagetes*, is very wide, both in the African and the French types—the first including plants with heights of 1ft to 3ft (30–90cm), the second 6–10in. (15–24cm). Good varieties of French marigolds include the 9in. (22cm) tall 'Honeycomb' with golden-yellow and brown, double, crested flowers and the superb 'Queen Sophia' of similar height, which has fully double red blooms prettily margined with golden-yellow. The double-flowered Boy O' Boy mixture, height 6in. (15cm), provides a mixture of colours, mahogany-red, golden-yellow, bright yellow and orange. If large blooms are to your liking then these you get in African marigolds like the Climax mixture, 3ft (90cm) tall, and the somewhat shorter 'Doubloon'. Gay Ladies mixture is but 1½ft (45cm) tall and provides excellent blooms of orange, golden-yellow and yellow colouring. Of the Afro-French hybrids an outstanding F₁ hybrid is 'Nell Gwynn', with large mahogany-red centred golden-yellow flowers borne on 1ft (30cm) stems.

I remember how impressed I was when I first saw the compact-growing strain of *Tagetes signata pumila* named Starfire a few years ago. I am still impressed, for these 10in. (24cm) tall plants provide a carpet of mahogany-red, golden yellow and lemon yellow with their tight-packed, small flowers. It is ideal for edging.

The perennial *Salvia farinacea* has a first-class variety named 'Victoria' which is grown to great effect as a half-hardy annual, and has been since its introduction in the late 1970s. It won a Floroselect bronze medal in that organisation's all-Europe trials in 1978. With its good foliage and bold spikes of violet-blue flowers borne on 2ft (60cm) stems, it is immensely alluring and is a plant for which many uses can be found in the garden.

The hardy biennials are a select little band which, for those who are prepared to take the trouble, have a great deal to offer. Sowing

Excelsior hybrids, a robust strain of the common foxglove *Digitalis purpurea* (see p. 58)

is done in a seed bed outdoors or in a cold frame during early summer to provide plants for transferring to a reserve bed and then moving to their flowering positions in autumn. One of the most useful and decorative of the biennials is undoubtedly *Cheiranthus allionii*, the Siberian wallflower, which produces its orange blooms on 1¼ft (37cm) stems from March until May and often until late June or early July. It has an excellent bright golden-yellow variety named 'Golden Bedder'. The *Cheiranthus × cheiri* (wallflower) varieties come in heights from 6in. to 1½ft (15–45cm) and in colours which embrace cream, yellows, many shades of pink, red and purple. These are fragrant, which the Siberian kind are not. One of the most effective of the taller kinds of wallflowers is 'Fire King', a bright scarlet, and another is 'Cloth of Gold', while of the low-growers mention must be made of the Tom Thumb mixture, some 9in. (23cm) tall.

Of the foxgloves (*Digitalis*) the Excelsior strain still reigns supreme, producing its lovely blooms in July and August on stems some 5ft (1.5m) high. It is the exquisite markings on the blooms, in their varied colours of cream, shades of pink and purple, which give them special appeal—and the blooms are, of course, borne all round the stems. There is also a lower-growing mixture named Foxy (some 3ft [90cm] tall) which can be raised as half-hardy annual by sowing the seeds under glass in early spring. All foxgloves love light shade.

In pansies, too, there is much to delight the gardener, from the Roggli Giant mixture, 6 to 8 inches (15–20cm) tall, to the Clear Crystals mixture and the Majestic Giants. In sweet williams my choice would be the dwarf Indian Carpet strain with its excellent colour range and height of about 6 to 9 inches (15–22cm). This needs full sun to give of its best.

The hollyhock, *Althaea rosea*, is, of course, a perennial but it is best treated as a biennial, and that notable strain, Summer Carnival, 5 to 6ft (1.5–1.8m) tall, can even be grown as a half-hardy annual to flower in the first year. This strain has double flowers of good quality in colours from red and pink to yellow and white. Also widely available from seed houses is the admirable Chater's Double Mixed strain, with a good colour range and a height similar to the last.

Vegetables growing in a raised bed

Vegetables and Fruit

What is surprising about vegetable growing is how much can be achieved in a small area. Cheap food is a receding memory, and on that score there is plenty of incentive to grow at least a little of one's food requirements. But the real pleasure for any gardener comes from growing and then enjoying at the table the best that the seedsman has to offer. The main problem is likely to be an aesthetic one. However well it is kept, a vegetable plot can detract from the overall effect of a garden, bearing in mind that it needs to be sited in an open position to give the good light which the majority of vegetables demand. On the other hand, it is often quite easy to provide a low screen which effectively overcomes the problem, either a fence on which permanent climbing plants can be grown, or, if a summer screen is quite sufficient, perhaps a row of french beans separating that part of the garden from the rest, Sweet peas or trained apples and pears can be used in the same way. The fact that quite of lot of vegetables can be successfully mixed with flowers should not be overlooked either. Vegetables can also look attractive grown in a raised bed.

Many herbs can be grown in containers, from mint (which needs restraining in any case), parsley and thyme to chives, which are always useful to have to hand.

It is most gardeners' ambition to have at least a few apples in the garden and possibly a few pears as well. If space is very tight then even dwarf bushes may be considered to take up too much room. So it comes down to trained specimens and of these the simple single-stem cordon is probably a better choice than the espalier form of training. Single-stem cordon apples and pears can be planted $2\frac{1}{2}$ to 3ft (75–90cm) apart in the row; trained on wires to form a screen between the vegetable plot and the rest of the garden they serve a very useful dual purpose. Apples need a good well-drained soil, not too heavy nor too light. Pears need rather warmer conditions to crop well and are not happy on heavier soils; they are more susceptible than apples, too, to frost damage at the flowering stage.

You must take note of the pollination requirements of whatever varieties you decide you would like to grow. Most apples are partially self-fertile, but for first-rate cropping there must be other compatible varieties nearby and flowering at the same time to effect cross pollination. On varieties, too, it is always a good idea to get local advice on which do well in your district.

If you have a south-facing wall with a clear space of 15ft (4.6m) or rather more, then consider growing espalier-trained pears —always allowing you have not earmarked this for one of the shrubs suggested earlier! For a north-facing wall, then it could be either a Morello cherry or a 'Victoria' plum; both are self-fertile.

If necessary, you can resort to growing most of the bush and cane fruits in containers, provided these are of large enough size; but clearly it is better to grow them in the open ground if this is possible. I would certainly try to find room for a couple of black currants—perhaps the mid-season variety 'Ben Lomond', heavy cropping and rather late flowering, which is helpful where frosts are concerned, or the later 'Baldwin'. Then there is the recently introduced 'Jet', a late-ripening variety which flowers late, with the advantage of missing the frosts—an excellent introduction from the East Malling Research Station. These are shallow-rooting and need a soil which will not dry out unduly while still being well-drained. Red currants, if you have room for them, can be planted at 5ft (1.5m) apart and I would suggest either 'Laxton's No. 1' or 'Red Lake', with the Dutch-raised variety 'Jonkheer van Tets' a strong contender for space with the first-mentioned, for these two are early cropping, with 'Red Lake' following on. Again, with space in mind, it is possible to grow red and white currants ('White Versailles' is the most freely available variety) as single or triple cordons. All do well in sunshine or light shade, but avoid sites open to cold winds.

If you can provide good soil (light soils are just not suitable) then the gooseberry to go for is 'Leveller', a yellow-fruited variety which you can use for both dessert and culinary purposes. More accommodating but susceptible to mildew is 'Whinham's Industry', another dual-purpose variety. 'Careless', the much-grown culinary variety, needs a good soil like 'Leveller' when it will crop splendidly, but it does make a large bush. Plant bushes 6ft (1.8m) apart each way.

Try and find space for at least a row of raspberries, the most rewarding soft fruit in my opinion. These do well in sunshine or light shade, given a moist, well-drained soil. Two varieties deserve special mention: the early 'Glen Clova' and 'Delight', which is a mid-season variety. Both are excellent croppers. However, 'Glen Clova' is susceptible to virus infection and for this reason should not be planted near other varieties. Then there is 'Zeva', a variety which can start to bear fruit in mid-August but which is mainly an autumn-fruiting variety, from September onwards. The plants should be set 1½ft (45cm) apart in the row.

Virtually everybody is interested in strawberries—at the consuming end in particular! They are a good crop for small gardens

'Red Lake', a mid-season red currant with good flavour, is a heavy cropper

in any case, but especially so in view of their suitability for growing in containers of various kinds (which must, of course, be deep and wide enough to hold enough good compost to meet their needs). I'm thinking especially of the barrel method of growing which can be such an attractive feature on a patio or paved sitting-out area. There are also proprietary tiered polypropylene pots in which strawberries can be grown on a patio. An early-cropping variety to consider growing is 'Pantagruella', and 'Cambridge Vigour' is a second-early variety with good flavour. Of the perpetual-fruiting (or remontant) varieties which continue fruiting into October, 'Gento' is to be recommended for flavour. Planted in a plot, set the plants 1½ft (45cm) apart in rows 2½ft (75cm) apart. They need good soil, good drainage, and access to plenty of sunshine.

A mixed border in early spring is set off by the greys of the stone wall and the tree bark

Right: The foliage of shrubs and herbaceous plants contrasts beautifully with the trunks of silver birch

Climbing and Wall Plants

GEORGE PRESTON

A small cottage garden offers surprising scope for a profusion
of colour and variety

Abutilon vitifolium needs a sheltered, sunny position to bloom from May to July

Introduction

Walls in a garden provide an opportunity for growing some special plants. Most walls provide shelter and so some extra warmth which may enable a plant to flourish in a district with a colder climate than its native country. For instance plants from the Mediterranean region will grow well in many parts of Britain against a south wall.

Climbing plants are those which have a natural means of supporting themselves, such as ivy (by its aerial roots), Boston ivy, often incorrectly called Virginia creeper (by its adhesive pads at the end of tendrils), honeysuckle (by its twining stems) or clematis (by its twining leaf stems).

The term is also used to cover many other plants which can be fixed to the wall artificially, for example tied in to a framework. Among these are the so-called climbing roses, which if grown in the open would make an untidy, sprawling bush like a blackberry, and also many less hardy shrubs which are trained against the wall, but which would make a bush or small tree if grown in the open.

Many of the climbing plants are indispensable to cover a large unsightly wall. Familiar examples are Boston ivy, *Parthenocissus*

Buddleja colvilei, a striking Himaylayan species which needs some protection in winter for its first few years (see p. 84)

tricuspidata, which provides a wonderful display of colour just before leaf fall, or the various forms of ivy, *Hedera helix*. Ivies, being evergreen, are valuable in providing colour all year round, those with yellow or white leaf variegations being of particular value in the dull days of winter. It would, however, be a waste of a good opportunity to use only plants such as ivy to cover a wall; a varied selection of other ornamental plants will bring interest at different times of the year.

The walls of houses or boundary walls provide ideal positions for climbing and other plants, including fruit trees, but one must always estimate the vigour and size to which the plant will eventually grow before planting, and consider the possible effect on the house. In most cases it is undesirable to have climbers growing too high, for with these it is difficult to prune and tie in the new growth; they may grow over windows, obscuring the view into the garden, and into the roof gutters causing blockages. Plants with a very strong root system can damage the foundations of the house if planted against a wall. Therefore the selection of the most suitable type of plant for the right position is most important.

On the whole, climbers, especially the more vigorous ones, are not as satisfactory as shrubs for covering walls of moderate height. In many cases they have a strong tendency to climb to the top of the wall leaving the lower parts bare. However, they can sometimes be trained along the top of the wall, leaving the lower spaces for shrubs. As I have already said, the great value of walls is not in providing accommodation for climbers alone, but also in affording conditions that enable beautiful shrubs, which are tender in the open ground, to grow successfully.

A colourful combination of *Parthenocissus tricuspidata* and pyracantha

——— Soil Preparation and Planting ———

For plants that are to be grown on boundary walls, no new soil or special preparations will be needed, especially if there is already a border in front of them, and where the soil is cultivated. Against the walls of houses or other buildings where the soil is often very poor, or where a gravelled or paved path is so close that there is little or no space for soil, then a considerable amount of preparation is necessary.

A space 1½ to 2ft (45–60cm) wide and as much deep should be made at the base of the wall and filled with good top soil. If this is not available, dig in some well-decayed manure, compost, leafmould, rotted straw or peat moss, any of which will be of considerable help in improving the soil. On a heavy clay soil, it may be necessary to add a certain amount of coarse drainage material, in addition to some well-decayed compost, leafmould or coarse peat moss which will help to increase the aeration and improve the drainage of the soil.

The ideal soil is a good light alluvial loam to which is added a quantity of decayed leaves or peat moss. If the soil is free from lime chalk, this mixture will suit a wide variety of plants, including the peat loving kinds.

Once the soil has been prepared and improved in structure, it should be levelled and firmed by careful treading before planting. When the plant is taken from its container, the roots should be disturbed as litttle as possible. When, as sometimes happens, a plant has remained in the pot too long and the roots have become very congested and formed a ball, try to open out the roots a little before planting, although too much root disturbance can check the plant's growth. Plants which have become very pot bound or root restricted rarely grow away so freely as those which have a less cramped root system. Make sure, when buying plants, that you choose those with deep green leaves rather than those showing early signs of starvation, such as leaf yellowing. It is important to make sure that the soil is thoroughly moist at planting time. If necessary, soak the plant overnight in a bucket of water before planting.

Dig a hole wide enough and deep enough to take the roots, and plant with the soil level at the same place on the stem as it was in the container. Firm the soil around the roots.

After planting, the young plant should be secured to a strong stake or some other means of support, to prevent it being blown about by the wind. A good mulch of well-rotted straw, manure, or garden compost round the base of the plant will help to conserve moisture and to prevent drying out of the soil during periods of drought. In its first growing season it may also be necessary to give the young plant a good watering in dry periods. Often the ground at the base of the wall or fence becomes very dry through lack of adequate rain, and it is essential to keep the soil damp by watering.

As most plants are grown and sold in containers, planting can be done at any time of the year although autumn or early spring is to be preferred.

Below: The slightly tender *Cytisus battandieri* benefits from wall protection (see p. 97)
Opposite above: *Carpentaria californica*, an evergreen flowering in June and July (see p. 87)
Opposite below left: *Cistus* × *purpureus*, one of the most decorative sun roses, is more likely to survive the winter against a wall (see p. 91)
Opposite below right: *Clematis* 'H. F. Young', one of the best blue flowered hybrids (see pp. 92–93)

Artificial Support

There are many climbers and shrubs which do not possess natural means of supporting themselves and therefore some type of artificial support has to be given. One of the commonest methods for brick walls is to use a specially stout type of non-rusting nails with strips of rubber backed pieces of canvas, strong cloth or other lasting material, such as plastic. Strong twine or tarred string can also be used in a similar way. The use of nails in the walls of dwelling houses or other buildings and walls is not altogether satisfactory and can be detrimental. Quite often during high winds, the extra weight on the branches caused by rain or heavy snowfalls will bring the supports, including the nails, from the wall. To avoid this the most satisfactory means of support is to fix stout galvanized wires horizontally to the wall, or in the case of twining climbers vertically, from 8 to 12in. (20–30cm) apart, held in position at regular intervals by hooked or eyelet-holed metal pins, known as vine eyes, driven into the wall. Strong galvanized hooks can also be used. Both types are available in shops, garden centres and nurseries.

Another method of support is a lattice work of narrow laths, painted or creosoted, and joined together in the form of frames, and wooden trellis work is equally effective. Both types can be easily fixed to the wall and held firm with the aid of wall plugs, screws or nails.

Strips of plastic-coated steel or wire netting fixed to the walls are also effective. This is very strong, resistant to rust and can be obtained in different mesh sizes and in various lengths. Much cheaper is the ordinary strong galvanized wire netting in various mesh sizes, but it is an advantage to give it a coat of bituminous paint before fixing to reduce rusting.

There are also other strong durable synthetic, polythene types of netting now available in various mesh sizes. They are easy to handle and cut to size, and are ideal supports for plants which do not make a heavy weight, such as *Lathyrus* (sweet pea) and *Ipomoea* (morning glory), which look very effective planted near the wall. Ordinary pea sticks can also be used.

A point to be remembered when dealing with vigorous climbers is that branches should be kept well clear of any gutters or drainpipes. The annual growth can easily be disentangled and

Above: The hardy *Abelia* × *grandiflora* flowers in late summer (see p. 83)
Below: *Crinodendron hookeranum* with its attractive crimson lanterns
(see p. 97)

removed, but with age the main stems of wisteria, for example, can be 6in. (5cm) or more in diameter, and can easily force a down-pipe or gutter away from the wall if allowed to grow behind it.

Using the above-mentioned methods of support some wall plants (including fruit trees, see pp. 127–130) are suitable for training into various forms, the most popular of which are fans and espaliers. The advantage of these forms is that the wall is well covered by the plant, which in turn is securely supported by wires, and this is less likely to be damaged in windy weather.

FAN TRAINING

This is a suitable method of training for a shrub such as *Ceanothus*, and all stone fruits, such as cherries, plums and peaches. During the first year after planting the main shoot is tied in vertically as it grows and the lateral shoots are fanned out to fill the available space as evenly as possible. In subsequent years the young shoots need to be tied in regularly during the spring and summer, and the previous season's growths should be pruned back after flowering. Annual regular pruning will maintain the shape of the mature plant.

ESPALIER

This method of training is suitable for ornamental shrubs, such as *Pyracantha*, and is often used for fruit trees. To train as an espalier, cut the young plant back to three good buds, with the two lower buds pointing in opposite directions. Tie the shoot from the top bud to a vertical support, and train the shoots from the other two buds along canes fixed at an angle of about 45° to the main stem. At the end of the growing season lower the two side branches to the horizontal wires and tie them in. Cut back the vertical leader to a bud about 18in. (45cm) above the lower arm, leaving two good buds to form the next horizontal arms. Cut back any surplus laterals on the main stem to three buds and prune back the lower horizontal arms by one-third, cutting to downward-facing buds. Repeat this process each year in the autumn until the shrub has filled the required space, and prune back the new terminal growths of the vertical and horizontal arms each summer, to keep the tree at its required size.

Above: The Mexican orange blossom, *Choisya ternata*, (see p. 91)
Below: *Coronilla glauca*, a useful member of the pea family, from southern Europe (see p. 97)

Feeding

Many wall plants, once they are established and making good root growth, become strong, vigorous growers and will benefit by regular annual feeding. This is especially necessary if they are growing in poor or light gravelly soil where the essential plant foods quickly become leached out, or where the plants are growing in a narrow border along a wall or near buildings where there is little soil and the nutrients become exhausted.

Any of the organic manures, such as hoof and horn, fish or meal bone, can be used to supply the nutrients. These can be obtained in various grades, although the coarser grades are slower acting and are best applied to the plant during the late winter or very early spring months. If these are difficult to obtain a general fertilizer is recommended. These contain the three major plant nutrients, nitrogen, potassium and phosphate. A good dressing should be scattered around the root of the plant and surrounding soil (about 2–3 oz. per square yard (56–85 g per m²)) and lightly forked into the top few inches of soil. This should preferably be done during showery weather or when the soil is moist. If the soil is dry, as often is the case against walls or near buildings where it is difficult for rain to penetrate, then it may be necessary to give it a good watering after the fertilizer has been applied.

Mulching or top dressing the soil with some well-rotted manure, compost, or leafmould not only keeps the soil and plant roots relatively warm in winter and cool and moist in the summer, but it can also provide some nutrients. The mulch can either be left on the surface or it can be forked lightly into the top few inches of soil during the winter months, but care should be taken not to expose the roots above the soil surface when forking. For plants which have just been transplanted it is better to leave the mulch on the surface to help retain moisture and keep the roots cool during the summer rather than fork it in.

With camellias and other plants which prefer plenty of leafmould and peat in the soil, there is nothing better than a good annual top dressing of decayed leaves which provide a natural feed for this particular class of plant.

Nasturtiums can dominate groupings along a wall or in a border where their trailing habit can be seen to advantage

Pruning

Plants which are grown on a wall usually have to be kept within certain limits. To do this the plants need a periodical, usually annual, pruning or training, which is dependent on two factors, the amount of space available and time of flowering. With regard to space this depends both on the area of wall available and on the distance the shrub can be allowed to grow out from the wall. Sometimes plants growing on walls are pruned too much and are kept too close against the wall; how much better to see a well-grown shrub with its branches standing out 1 or 2ft (30–60cm) from the wall. It is better to choose a plant which is amenable to training, rather than having to keep continually pruning.

The time to prune depends on the time of year that the plant flowers and the type of growth. Climbers and shrubs can be divided roughly into two groups; those that flower on the current season's shoots, generally from midsummer onwards to the autumn, and those that flower from March to June on shoots made the previous summer.

In the first group pruning consists of cutting back the shoots that have flowered, if possible to a dormant bud near the base. This should be done in late winter or early spring (February–March) so as to give the plant the longest possible period for growing before flowering later in the year; examples of this group are *Clematis* × *jackmanii* types, some types of *Buddleja*, and *Caryopteris*.

The second group includes those that flower on the growth made in the previous summer; pruning should be done immediately after flowering, cutting back the strong growths which have just flowered to encourage new shoots. These will produce buds to flower in the following season. Sufficient young shoots should also be left, on which flower buds will be formed for the following year. Examples of this group are *Ceanothus*, *Buddleja davidii*, *Forsythia*, *Prunus triloba* and *Clematis montana*.

This hard annual pruning is not necessary for all plants. There are quite a number of plants which are not vigorous growers and make comparatively little growth every year, and they require little or no pruning, certainly no annual pruning, only tying in the new growth as it develops. Young plants that are in the early stages of being trained up a wall need only very light pruning each year to encourage branching and stimulate more growth on

'Mrs James Mason' in the vigorous, fully hardy *Clematis montana* group (see p.93)

which the framework of the plant is built up. It is only when it has reached its maximum height and allotted space that it may be necessary to prune harder.

For plants which are grown primarily for their foliage or autumn colour, such as vines or variegated shrubs, the time of pruning is less important. The most favourable times are winter for deciduous plants and early spring for evergreens, with possibly a second pruning in August to thin out redundant or overcrowded shoots.

While pruning is being done it is wise to cut out any dead or weak shoots and to check and renew where necessary old or weak ties which support the main framework. It is also important to make a regular inspection of all plants during the growing season and tie in new shoots. Often, uncontrolled growths become intertwined with one another, making it difficult to sort them out at the end of the growing season.

Fuller details of pruning requirements are given in *Pruning Ornamental Shrubs*, also published in the Wisley Handbook Series.

Prunus triloba should be cut back immediately after flowering (see p.114)

Winter Protection

One of the reasons for growing a plant against a wall is to give some extra protection to plants that would be killed or damaged by a winter in the open. Some of these plants may need additional cover in their first few winters, until they become established.

It is difficult to cover completely half-hardy or tender shrubs which have grown to more than 5ft (1.5m) high, unless it is something really very special. The main aim with established plants is to protect the lower parts of the stem and branches up to about 3ft (90cm) from the ground, from which new growth can develop in spring if the unprotected parts of the plant are injured or killed by frost.

The time to put on the covering depends on the weather. Severe weather before December or even January is unusual, and the longer that covering is delayed the more acclimatized to low temperatures the plants will become. But, to be on the safe side, the plants should be covered by the end of November. Remove the protection in early March, when the weather has usually started to warm up.

Probably the best and most convenient material to use is dried bracken that has been cut in late autumn. If this is not obtainable short straw is quite effective. Tuck the material lightly in around the lower branches, allowing air to circulate freely through the material so that it remains relatively dry at all times; this is an important factor during frost. A few stakes and some twine will help to keep the material in position. The use of dead stems such as Michaelmas daisies, *Solidago* and similar material cut from the herbaceous border, can also be effectively used in the same way.

Another method quite often adopted and one which can be used for several successive winters, is to place a thick layer of bracken, straw or other similar material between lengths of small mesh galvanized wire netting or polythene film, which is firmly tied together to keep the material in position. The netting can then be cut into various lengths as required and held in position by a few stakes. Pieces of sacking or coconut matting can be cut into the required lengths and used in a similar way.

With plants of a semi-prostrate habit the material can be lightly worked in and around the stems and if necessary held in position with a few short upright stakes.

Above: A mixture of annuals and perennials clothing a wall
Below left: *Abutilon megapotamicum*, an evergreen shrub from Brazil for a sheltered corner (see p. 83). Below right: *Actinidia chinensis*, the Kiwi fruit, a vigorous climber, grown in particular for its handsome leaves (see p. 83)

Perennial Climbing and Wall Plants

Abelia floribunda is the most tender and the most beautiful of the abelias, having rosy red, pendulous, funnel-shaped flowers borne on long arching stems during June and July. For a south or west wall this shrub with its shining leaves is most attractive. **Abelia × grandiflora**, which is hardier, has white and pink blossoms, and flowers from July until the autumn; it has a very graceful habit and is most useful flowering so late in the season. Both species mentioned are reasonably slow growing but eventually reach a height of 5 to 6ft (1.5–1.8m) and more in very sheltered localities. It is hardy except in severe winters (see p. 73).

Abeliophyllum distichum originates from Korea, and is related to *Forsythia* (see p. 99). It is a comparatively slow growing, hardy but dainty deciduous twiggy shrub, which grows to about 4ft (1.2 m) high. The small flowers are fragrant, white tinged pink and freely produced on short racemes. Unfortunately it starts to flower at the end of January and is liable to be damaged by frost; on a south wall there is less danger of this.

Abutilon megapotamicum, although a native of Brazil, makes a very graceful evergreen shrub for growing in a sheltered position, where it will come through an average winter unharmed. It is an advantage to give some protection around the base of the plant, using either dried bracken fronds, straw, or similar material, as a precaution. The bright red and yellow pendulous flowers are produced on long slender arching growths from the leaf axils, throughout the summer. There is also a variegated form which has leaves blotched with bright yellow.

Abutilon vitifolium is an altogether larger, more upright shrub, which requires a sheltered, sunny position. The saucer-shaped flowers, which are pale to deep mauve and continue in bloom from May to July, are well set off by the vine-shaped greyish leaves. In recent years it has been crossed with *A. ochsenii*, a weaker growing species from Chile but with beautifully shaped violet flowers. The hybrid, × *suntense* is as vigorous as *A. vitifolium* and hardier. The flowers have the better shape and deeper violet of *A. ochensii*. All three plants benefit from wall protection in colder gardens but are unsuitable for training on a wall (see p. 66).

Actinidia chinensis, a deciduous climber introduced from

China in 1900, is very vigorous and will if required grow up a tree. It is worth growing for its large, handsome heart-shaped leaves. Its creamy buff-yellow flowers are sometimes followed in Britain by brown, edible fruits the size of an egg, sold as Kiwi fruit. Both sexes are necessary to obtain fruits (see p. 82).

Actinidia kolomikta is a deciduous species from China, Japan and Manchuria, which is not as vigorous as some other species. It is well worth growing for the attraction of its leaves which when fully developed have a large area of pink and white variegation at the tips.

Akebia is an Asiatic genus of two species of vigorous, deciduous climbers with racemes of small, dark purple or purple-brown flowers, which in some years are followed by violet, sausage-shaped fruits. In *A. lobata* the leaves are composed of three leaflets while those of *A. quinata* are made up of five leaflets. In both species the foliage is elegant, but they require space.

Ampelopsis brevipedunculata, a luxuriant climber from eastern Asia, has deeply lobed and bristly leaves like those of the hop. It is attractive in autumn with its branches of small bright blue grapes. Its clone 'Elegans' (also known as *A. heterophylla* var. *variegata*) is far less strong growing and has handsome leaves which are mottled white and pink, with pinkish young shoots. This also needs a more sheltered position and is better suited to the milder counties. It is sometimes sold as a houseplant.

Aristolochia macrophylla (also known as *A. sipho*) is a plant grown chiefly for its foliage effect. It is commonly called Dutchman's pipe on account of the flowers being shaped like a dutch pipe. They are about 1 to 2in. (2–5cm) long, tubular, inflated and yellowish green in colour; the flat expanding lobes at the end of the flowers are brownish purple. It is a very vigorous climber, and is useful for quick coverage. The large, kidney-shaped leaves are deciduous.

Berberidopsis corallina, sometimes known as the coral plant, is beautiful when well grown. As a native of Chile it is not really hardy and only suited for the milder parts of the country. It needs a very sheltered and preferably a cool shady position, in a rich, lime-free soil. It is an evergreen shrub with heart shaped, dark green leaves and large pendent globular coral red flowers produced in the axils of the uppermost leaves in beautiful drooping racemes. It is not self supporting and it is necessary therefore to tie the leading shoots to some sort of support.

Buddleja colvilei, which originates from the Himalayas, will reach almost tree-like dimensions in cultivation. It has large lance-shaped leaves and drooping panicles of substantial rose to rosy crimson bell-shaped flowers, which are borne on mature

Ceanothus (see p.87) prefers a sunny south-facing wall, but will accept those facing east or west

growths. It should never be pruned annually or cut back in early spring as is the case with the well-known *B. davidii (variabilis)*. Care is needed, and space, if it is to be trained on a wall. It is admirable when planted in the angle of two walls where it should be allowed to develop without restraint. It is tender when young and requires winter protection until well established (see p.67).

The genus **Camellia** contains a wide variety of excellent flowering evergreen shrubs, suited not only for woodland planting but also useful for growing on walls. There is space here to deal only with a number of the less hardy species and some of the more recent hybrids which, because they flower when frosts are prevalent, derive benefit from the shelter of walls. *Camellia cuspidata* has a distinctive habit, with slender growths, small white flowers and copper-tinted young growths. It has been largely superseded by its hybrid 'Cornish Snow', which has rather larger flowers produced in greater profusion from March onwards, while retaining much of the quiet charm of its parent.

There are innumerable cultivars of the Japanese *C. sasanqua* grown in its native land and such warm climates as that of California. In this country one cultivar alone, 'Nurumi-gata', with flowers resembling those of the Christmas rose, blooms with sufficient regularity to warrant its use on valuable wall space. It is of value as it produces its attractive flowers from October onwards.

Two related Chinese species *C. reticulata* and *C. saluenensis* show considerable variation in size of leaf and in shape and tone of their pink flowers. Except in very mild areas wall protection is essential if they are to succeed and, like the species and hybrids already mentioned, they are well worth the shelter of a west or north-west wall, particularly where an unusual plant is desired. A hybrid between these two species, 'Francie L' is well suited to training on walls and bears beautiful large, deep rose-coloured flowers.

Camellia saluenensis crossed with *C. japonica*, has produced a race of hybrids known collectively as *C. × williamsii*, with almost unparalleled freedom of flower, surprising hardiness and other good qualities. They start to flower when young plants, and most of them have the advantage of shedding their flowers as soon as they fade or become damaged. In the south they do not need the protection of a wall, but as they flower when frost is prevalent the shelter of a wall may ensure a successful display of flowers and their pinks and rosy reds will lighten many a dull wall. The following are some of the best cultivars:

'Donation' upright habit.

'E. G. Waterhouse', upright habit, formal double, pink.

'George Blandford', low, spreading, early, but long in flower, semi-double, rosy red.

'J. C. Williams', horizontal branching, single flat, blush pink.

'Lady Gowrie', compact, vigorous, large semi-double pink.

'November Pink', open habit, earliest to flower, but continuously in flower, single, funnel-shaped, pink.

'Parkside', open, spreading, single, clear pink.

'St Ewe', erect, single, funnel-shaped, rosy red.

Camellia × *williamsii* 'Donation' is considered to be one of the most outstanding camellias. However, equally outstanding is 'Leonard Messel', in which the semi-double pink flowers have a hint of coral. Although a hybrid of the tender *C. reticulata* with *C.* × *williamsii* 'Mary Christian', it is apparently as hardy as 'Donation'.

All camellias like a good moisture-retentive soil, well drained, but free from lime, and preferably one to which peat or leafmould has been added; they will not succeed on a chalk soil. Little pruning is required apart from an occasional thinning of overcrowded growth, dead wood and regular tying in of new growth. (See also the Wisley Handbook *Camellias*.)

Campsis is yet another genus of vigorous, deciduous climbers, which can be spectacular when covered with orange or orange-red, trumpet-shaped flowers. Unfortunately in Britain we do not enjoy sufficient regular hot summers to produce flowers in profusion and they are perhaps better when seen in southern Europe. *Campsis radicans* supports itself by aerial roots and may attain a height of 30–40ft (9–12cm). There is a hybrid 'Madame Galen' which is hardier than its parents. (*C. grandiflora* and *C. radicans*) and bears salmon-red flowers. Campsis should be planted against a south or west-facing wall.

Carpenteria californica is an evergreen shrub with a neat habit of growth reaching a height of 5 to 6ft (1.5–1.8m). It requires a sunny position (preferably facing south) and good drainage. The large white flowers contrasting with the golden anthers, are borne in June and July in terminal clusters of from three to six. These are 2 to 3in. (5–7cm) wide with five rounded petals (see p. 71).

The genus **Ceanothus** contains mostly evergreen shrubs with flowers of varying shades of blue and purple. They are native to the warm regions of California, Colorado and New Mexico where they get plenty of sunshine and hot dry conditions. Most of them prefer a light, well-drained sandy soil on a sunny south wall, but also succeed on walls facing west or east.

One of the most popular is *C.* × *veitchianus*, a spreading bush up to 10ft (3m) high, with small roundish glossy green leaves and dense heads of bright blue flowers produced during May and

June. *Ceanothus rigidus* has small glossy, holly-shaped leaves and deep purplish blue flowers borne in great profusion during April and May.

Another easy species is *C. dentatus* which has small oval leaves, bright green above but covered with a close grey felt on the underside. The brilliant blue flowers are produced in clusters in May. Another distinct plant, grown under the name of *Ceanothus impressus*, is considered by some to be a variety of *C. dentatus*. It is very close growing, with very small leaves and rich blue flowers. It quickly attains a height of 10 to 12ft (3–3.6m).

A very fine, early flowering species worthy of its place is *C. thyrsiflorus* which is a stronger growing type with larger, more rounded, glossy green leaves about $1\frac{1}{2}$ to 2in. long and 1in. wide (5×2.5cm). The pale blue flowers are borne in clusters on long stalks from the leaf axils of the previous season's growth.

Equally attractive and vigorous but inclined to be less hardy is *C. griseus*. Its large oval shaped leaves are similar in size but dull grey green on the under surface; the flowers are a pale lilac shade making it a very attractive plant when in flower in May.

All those *Ceanothus* which flower in early spring do so on the growth which has been made the previous season. It is therefore very important to carry out any pruning which may be necessary immediately after flowering, shortening back the growths which have flowered to within a few inches of their base.

There are a few other species which flower in summer on growth made during the current season; for this group, which includes the popular 'Gloire de Versailles', pruning has to be done in early spring (March-April). Strong shoots are shortened back to two or three buds from the base.

Celastrus orbiculatus, a twining climber, is related to the spindle berries and like them has small, highly decorative yellow and red fruits. It is very robust and apart from the necessity to plant both male and female plants, requires a lot of space. The leaves turn yellow before falling.

The genus **Chaenomeles** is a useful group of deciduous shrubs, which although perfectly hardy, look very attractive when grown as wall plants. Given a warm sunny position they will often come into flower early in the spring, and will also succeed in conditions of partial shade, such as on north-east or west walls. Regular pruning of wall plants will improve their flowering. Cut back the side shoots to two or three buds aftrer flowering is over.

Chaenomeles speciosa (the well-known early flowering "japonica") is very vigorous; there are different kinds producing flowers in all shades of red, pink or white from March or early

Clematis is ideal for covering a wall, although support must be given to
which the leaf tendrils can cling

A wall protects a border from the wind and retains heat

May. Some clones such as 'Simonii' are dwarfer with more pendulous branches and flat, blood red or scarlet flowers. They and *C. japonica* have a spreading habit and do not normally grow more than 3ft (90cm), thus being ideal for planting against low walls or under windows where wall space is restricted.

A race of hybrids, named *C. × superba*, has been raised by crossing *C. japonica* with *C. speciosa* and can be trained up to 6ft (1.8 m) or more on walls. Often clones of the species and hybrids are grouped together in catalogues. They include 'Crimson and Gold', red with golden stamens; 'Moerloosii', pink and white; 'Knap Hill Scarlet', orange-red; 'Nivalis', pure white; 'Phylis Moore', almond-pink; 'Rowallane', blood-red (see p. 101).

Chimonanthus praecox, the well-known winter sweet, is a very old and delightful shrub introduced from China as far back as 1766, since when it has been a great favourite because of its sweetly scented flowers. Although perfectly hardy it benefits from the warmth of a sunny wall. It flowers from December and intermittently until March depending on the weather. The flowers are borne on the previous summer's growth, with the outer petals greenish yellow, the inner ones purplish, and each about one inch across. They have no particular beauty but are valued for their fragrance and early flowering. The clone 'Luteus' has larger flowers. Regular pruning is not needed but long shoots may be pruned no later than March.

Choisya ternata, Mexican orange blossom, is another useful shrub for planting where it can receive plenty of sun and shelter from cold east winds which may damage the growth in some winters. It is an evergreen of rounded bushy habit 6 to 9ft (1.8–2.7 m) high, requiring ample space to develop. The leaves are glossy green, 3 to 6in. (7–15cm) long, composed of two to three leaflets. The white fragrant flowers are borne in clusters of three to five during April and May on the previous year's growth, and occasionally again during the late summer (see p. 75).

Another very useful and decorative group of sun-loving, evergreen plants is **Cistus**; all appreciate a hot sheltered position and thrive in light well-drained soil. Most are native to the Mediterranean, and as one would expect may suffer badly during a very severe winter. Most flower from May to July.

One of the most striking is *C. × purpureus* which has leathery leaves and large bright rose-purple flowers with a conspicuous chocolate basal blotch. It makes a rounded bush up to 5 to 6ft (1.5–1.8m) high (see p. 71).

Cistus ladanifer is a beautiful, erect species up to 6ft (1.8m) high, with sticky, lance-shaped leaves. The flowers are white, with a crimson zoning at the base.

Cistus × pulverulentus, sometimes called 'Sunset', makes a compact shrub of 2 to 3ft (60–90cm) high, with grey-green hairy leaves, and rosy pink flowers about 2in. (5cm) wide.

Cistus × skanbergii forms a dense twiggy shrub up to 4ft (1.2 m) high, with grey-green leaves and small shell pink flowers in terminal clusters.

These are but a few of a large group. Their disadvantage is that they are short-lived, although new plants can easily be raised from cuttings. These are best taken in August after flowering using short soft wooded nodal cuttings 2 to 3in. (5–7cm) in length and rooted in sandy soil (1 part soil to 3 parts of silver sand), or some other rooting medium, in a cold or if possible a slightly heated frame.

There is no cultivated genus of climbers to equal **Clematis**, a very useful and extensive group of wall plants which, when in flower, provide some of the most beautiful effects one could wish for in a garden. The various types provide blooms for many months during the summer starting from June until the end of September, but although they are perfectly hardy, the young growth may occasionally be damaged by late spring frosts. They provide a great variety of colour particularly among the hybrids of the large flowered types ranging from white, blue, purple, and mauve to red and pink. They constitute the most important section of the genus.

These hybrids are not difficult to grow, succeeding in a retentive but well-drained, loamy, calcareous soil, although all of them – including many of the species – will thrive quite well in soil which does not contain lime. The best time to plant is during the autumn, in October or November; if this is not possible, plant in early spring before new growth starts. Once planted they should be left undisturbed at the roots and when established will continue and flower regularly every year. They are all sun lovers, but the lower part of the main stem should preferably be shaded; this can be done by planting near the base of the plant a dwarf shrub which will cast some light shade and allow the clematis to grow up through it. With the exception of more tender species like *C. armandii* they generally do well in every aspect except dense shade.

The selection of these hybrids is a matter of personal choice. However, among the best are 'Barbara Dibley', pansy violet with petunia bars; 'Barbara Jackman', soft petunia with plum colour bars; 'Beauty of Worcester', deep violet blue; 'Captain Thuilleaux' cream with deep pink bars; 'Comtesse de Bouchaud', soft mauve pink; 'Duchess of Edinburgh', double white; 'Elsa Spath', deep lavender; 'Hagley Hybrid', deep shell pink; 'H.F. Young,

Wedgwood blue; 'Huldine', translucent white with pink bands on the reverse; 'Jackmanii', deep violet; 'Lasurstern', rich blue; 'Marie Boisselot', pure white; 'Mrs Cholmondely', lavender blue; 'Nellie Moser', mauve pink with carmine bands; 'The President', deep violet; 'Perle d'Azur', pale blue; 'Ville de Lyon', deep carmine-red. Those cultivars with contrasting bars or bands are best grown with a north-west aspect if the colours are not to fade in the sun (see p. 71).

Among the large number of species in cultivation there are some which I consider just as attractive and as easy to grow. Foremost is *Clematis montana*, probably one of the most beautiful Asiatic deciduous species ever to have been introduced. It is very vigorous, growing 15 to 20ft (4.5–6m) high and even more if allowed to do so. Its white flowers are borne in great profusion during May and June in axillary clusters on long growths made the previous year. There are also several very good forms, such as *rubens*, with the same vigorous growth and rosy pink flowers; 'Elizabeth', large pearly pink flowers, sweetly scented; 'Tetrarose', extra large pink flowers which retain their colour to maturity, followed by purplish green foliage; and the variety *wilsonii* which has very large white flowers produced much later in the season. Any pruning to be done to these early flowering types should not be done until after flowering, cutting back the shoots that have flowered almost to their base.

Another species worth growing is *C. chrysocoma*, with white flowers tinged pink opening in May and June, and quite often again in late summer on the new growth. The leaves, flower stalks and very young shoots are covered with a fine yellowish silky down which gives the plant an attractive appearance. One of its chief merits for a small garden is that it is less rampant than *Clematis montana*.

Clematis armandii is a beautiful Chinese species, a strong grower well worth planting for its handsome evergreen, dark green leathery trifoliate leaves and cluster of creamy white sweetly scented flowers opening in early spring. It is liable to injury in severe winters and therefore demands a sheltered sunny position on a wall. It requires very little pruning, but care should be taken when tying in new growth which is often brittle and breaks readily. There are two very good cultivars, 'Snowdrift' a good white, and 'Apple Blossom' which has broad petals delicately shaded pink.

Where space is limited *Clematis macropetala* is a very charming species to grow. It has a much more slender type of growth ultimately reaching a height of 6 to 10ft (1.8–3m). The flowers are solitary on growth made in the previous year, usually powder blue in colour, although seedlings vary considerably. There is a cultivar called 'Markham's Pink' which has very nice pink flowers and is well worth growing. Although this species is quite hardy it does look most attractive when trained on a wall, fence or pergola while in some gardens it seems to thrive better if given a semi-shady position, supporting itself on some other shrub.

Another very delightful deciduous Chinese species is *C. tangutica*. It is quite hardy, but well suited for training up a wall, or planted near some other light shrub or climber where its slender growth can ramble at will. It produces an abundance of solitary yellow flowers from July onwards, followed by attractive round feathery seed heads. Another yellow flowered species is *Clematis tibetana* subsp. *vernayi* (LS&E No. 13342) known as 'Orange Peel' with four thick, waxy yellow sepals.

The method of pruning depends (a) on the position and space they are intended to occupy and (b) on their time and mode of flowering. The early flowering types such as *C. montana* and its varieties, *C. armandii* and *C. macropetala*, do not need regular pruning, but, if necessary, are pruned as soon as possible after flowering. The amount of pruning is related to the space the plant is to occupy. Once the allotted space has been filled then it may be necessary to cut hard back to old woody stems particularly if the plant becomes top heavy and growth a tangled mass. All new growth made after pruning should be carefully tied into position where required.

The later flowering types like *C. × jackmanii* and *C. lanuginosa* cultivars, which flower on the current year's growth, are pruned during February, cutting back the old flowering stems to growth buds which will by this time be large enough to show which parts of the stems are alive or dead. Occasionally it is advisable to cut a small proportion of the stems well back so that the new shoots will be stimulated to grow from the lower parts of the plant which so often remain bare. Great care should be taken when tying in new shoots, which, being soft and brittle, are easily broken. (See also the Wisley Handbook *Clematis*.)

Clianthus puniceus is a slightly tender shrub from New Zealand, and therefore prefers a south or west-facing wall. If provided with warmth and a well-drained soil it will produce bright red flowers, looking somewhat like a lobster's claw, during June and July. Winter protection, using bracken, straw or polythene is advisable in northern areas of Britain. It grows to about 8ft (2.4m) and can be propagated by seed sown in spring, or by cuttings taken during the summer.

Another very useful low growing shrub of 2 to 3ft (60–90cm) is **Convolvulus cneorum**, a south European species, with lovely

Forsythia 'Lynwood' (see p.28) is a favourite for its cheery colour in early spring

The bright yellow flowers of *Jasminum nudiflorum*, winter jasmine (see p.103), combine here with sprays of the red berries of *Cotoneaster horizontalis*

silver foliage which makes a good foil to the white and blush-pink, funnel-shaped flowers in summer. It loves a hot dry sunny position in well drained soil. I have seen it growing and flowering with great freedom on chalky soil.

Coronilla glauca belongs to the pea family and is from south Europe. It is an attractive plant for a warm sunny sheltered position, making a neat bush up to 5ft (1.5m) high with clusters of rich yellow pea-shaped flowers which contrast with the glaucous green pinnate leaves. It is a plant with a long flowering period from April until June and quite often a second flush in autumn (see p. 75).

Cotoneaster horizontalis always makes a charming shrub in whatever position it is placed. Normally if grown in the open it spreads horizontally but it is attractive when allowed to grow upwards and trained against a wall to show off its characteristic 'herringbone' habit of branching. Each autumn it can be relied upon to give masses of bright red berries with rich autumn foliage. It is a good plant for a north or east facing wall.

With the right growing conditions, particularly in the milder parts, and sufficient space, every endeavour should be made to grow at least one specimen of **Crinodendron**. The most attractive species is the evergreen *Crinodendron hookerianum*, it grows into a large shrub that produces urn-shaped flowers during early summer which hang from the branches like crimson lanterns in contrast to the deep green lance-shaped leaves. It requires a cool moist lime-free soil of loam and peat, and needs a very sheltered warm wall shaded from the hot midday sun (see p. 73).

The Moroccan **Cytisus battandieri** is a vigorous, loose-growing shrub, or small tree, up to 15ft (4.5m) high, which although it is hardy in the southern counties, is an excellent plant for training on sunny walls. The leaves are laburnum-like and covered with a silky, silvery sheen. The yellow flowers are scented of pineapple and are carried in erect cone-shaped clusters on the current year's growth in June or July. It does not need hard pruning, and only unnecessary or dead wood should be removed. It is usually raised from seed, which is often set freely, and seedlings may take a considerable number of years before flowering. They also show some variation, some being more prolific in flowering than others (see p. 70).

Dendromecon rigida is a beautiful, evergreen, rather tender shrub which needs a warm, sunny wall. It requires a light, well-drained soil, and, if happy, can reach a height of up to 15ft (4.6 m). The bright yellow, poppy-like flowers are borne from spring to autumn.

A plant from South America is **Desfontainea spinosa**, a

very large beautiful evergreen shrub with small holly-like leaves. The large conspicuous red and orange tubular flowers are produced singly from the leaf axils from July to September. It will come through most winters unharmed in the milder counties of the south and west, and many fine specimens are to be seen about the country growing against a wall. It appears to thrive on a wall sheltered from hot sun and in cool lime-free soil (see p. 133).

Eccremocarpus scaber is a charming semi-woody climber growing 5 to 6ft (1.5–1.8m) high in favourable conditions. The plant climbs by the tendrils produced by the pinnate leaves. From June onwards long racemes of up to a dozen bright orange, yellow or red tubular flowers about 1in. (2.5cm) long are produced until late in the summer (see p. 104).

It was introduced into this country late in 1824, and not being completely hardy is well suited for growing on a south or west wall. In some colder areas, young seedlings may have to be raised each year. This is easily done by sowing early in the spring in a little heat, hardening off and then planting out in a permanent position to flower the same season.

Another distinct member of the pea family is **Erythrina crista-galli**, perhaps better known as the coral tree; it likes a warm sunny position against a wall. Established plants have a thick woody rootstock from which are produced strong annual shoots 6 to 8ft (1.8–2.4m) long; these bear oval leathery leaflets more or less glaucous green, terminating in a large inflorescence of conspicuous deep scarlet flowers in autumn. To encourage strong healthy flowering shoots the following season, these long annual growths should be cut hard back to within a few inches of the base of the rootstock each spring before new growth begins. Being a native of Brazil this plant is only half-hardy in most parts of the country, and therefore the rootstock must be covered with some form of protection against severe frost (see p. 101).

Of the many attractive hybrids of the South American genus **Escallonia**, the finest and most suitable as a wall shrub is E. × iveyi. It has dark green, oval leaves, which are typically glossy, and large, pyramidal panicles of white flowers in late summer and autumn. It can make a large rounded shrub after many years, but there is a fine specimen some 6 to 7ft (1.8–2.1m) high growing on a south wall at Kew, which has survived many winters.

Euonymus fortunei var. **radicans** is a creeping shrub which will grow up to 15ft (4.5m) on a house wall. The plant is as useful as ivy in covering large areas of wall, and will grow in the same sort of conditions, growing well in sunny or shaded positions. It is grown as a foliage plant, and in its climbing state does not produce flowers.

There is also a variegated cultivar 'Variegatus', which has a white band along both sides of the leaves. It is a colourful plant in spring when the new leaves are produced. There is another variegated cultivar called 'Silver Queen'.

Fabiana imbricata is a very charming evergreen with heath-like foliage belonging to the potato family. It is a Chilean shrub for a warm sunny position, having slender racemes of long, narrow, white, tubular-shaped flowers each $\frac{1}{2}$ to $\frac{3}{4}$in. (12–19mm) long produced in June.

I well remember a fine specimen of it, 6 to 8ft (1.8–2.4m) high, growing and flowering freely each year, on a sheltered west wall at the Cambridge Botanic Garden. There it survived several hard winters unharmed, in a light gravelly soil containing a high percentage of lime. Equally attractive and of similar appearance is the variety *violacea* with flowers of a pale shade of mauve, which is hardier in some localities.

Feijoa sellowiana is an evergreen shrub, which, being slightly tender, prefers a south or south-west facing wall. It will grow up to 15ft (4.6m) and has dark, grey-green leaves, which, together with the flower stalks, are covered with a white felt. The flowers are red and white, with conspicuous crimson stamens, and these are borne in July. *Feijoa* can be propagated by means of cuttings taken in July or August, and raised in a heated greenhouse.

All species and hybrids of **Forsythia** in cultivation are perfectly hardy but one species, *F. suspensa*, is particularly effective when it flowers in early spring, if trained on a north or east facing wall. It will grow up to 15ft (4.5m) high and requires ample space if it is to be well trained. Its variety *sieboldii* has golden yellow flowers and those of var. *atrocaulis* are pale lemon yellow, which are most attractive hanging from the black stems.

The training and pruning of a young forsythia to cover a given area of wall space requires several years of patience, although this can also be said of other plants as well. In its early stages it involves careful pruning to selected growth buds to encourage strong healthy stems or leaders which will form the framework to tie in these strong growths to the wall during their growing period in whichever direction they are required, in the same way as one would train a young fruit tree up a wall (see *espalier*, p. 74).

Immediately after flowering prune the leading shoots back to about half their length to two or three selected buds which will produce further strong shoots which are tied in during the current year. This same process of pruning and tying in subsequent growth is repeated until the whole allotted space is filled. In the meanwhile lateral growths will have been bearing flowers, and these should be pruned back immediately after flowering to a bud within 2 or 3in. (5–7cm) of the base of that year's growth. This method of pruning is repeated each year after flowering to encourage new flowering growth, and it also helps to keep the plant reasonably confined to the wall and prevents a lot of untidy straggly growth. This training and method of pruning can also be applied to *Prunus triloba* (see p. 114), *Chaenomeles* (see p. 88) and similar spring flowering plants.

The two species of **Fremontodendron** (until recently called *Fremontia*), *F. californicum* and *F. mexicanum*, are distinctly tender but well worth growing where there is space on a warm, sunny wall, for they often reach the roof in the south west. They are semi-deciduous with three-lobed leaves, felted on the under surface as are the stems with rust-coloured hairs, and slightly greyed above. The flowers appear in the summer, their great beauty being really bright yellow, rounded calyces, which in *F. mexicanum* are narrow and rather star-like.

There is now a hybrid of American origin between these two species called 'California Glory'; it is a strong, free flowering plant worth growing and is widely available through the trade; it is also hardier.

Garrya elliptica is an evergreen bushy shrub vigorous in growth once established, 6 to 10ft (1.8–3m) high when grown on a wall, and higher in the milder parts of the country. Its leaves are more or less round, dark shiny green above and grey-woolly beneath, from the axils of which are produced long slender hanging male catkins 3 to 5in. (7.6–12cm) in length, on which the greenish silvery clusters of flowers are formed. These catkins look most attractive from November to February at a time of the year when there is little of interest in the garden. The catkins of the female flowers, which are on separate plants, are much shorter and less attractive.

I have also seen good healthy specimens growing on walls with a northern and east facing aspect which is rather surprising considering the species is a native of California and Oregon.

Cistus and *Halimium* are closely related and have produced the bigeneric hybrid × **Halimiocistus wintonensis**. It is a very useful plant for the front of a border at the foot of a sunny wall as it only grows about 2ft (60cm) high and its grey leaves and large white flowers with a maroon and yellow basal blotch are attractive.

Halimium lasianthum is a similar plant, rather taller and with small silvery leaves, among which the yellow flowers, each with a chocolate blotch at the base, are very pretty. In the variety *concolor* the flowers are without blotches and about 2in. (5cm) across as are those of the species and hybrid (see p. 104).

There are innumerable species and hybrids of the genus **Hebe**.

Above: *Erythrina crista-galli*, the coral tree, from Brazil (see p. 98)
Below left: *Chaenomeles × superba* 'Knap Hill Scarlet', with abundant, large, brilliant red flowers, is one of several hybrids in this group (see p. 91)
Below right: *Fremontodendron californicum* is an unusual summer flowering shrub but not reliably hardy

All are shrubby and evergreen, some are almost prostrate and others are big, bold shrubs with large leaves.

Among these large leaved hebes there is a group with colourful flowers generally known as *speciosa* hybrids, which are well worth growing if space is available under the shelter of a wall. There they will flower all summer long and form round bushes about 5 to 6ft (1.5–1.8m) high. Among the best of them are 'Alicia Amherst', deep purple; 'Gloriosa', bright pink; 'Purple Queen', bronze-tinted foliage, rosy purple; and 'Simon Delaux', rich crimson. All are somewhat tender.

Of the species of moderate height *H. hulkeana* is the most attractive with lustrous, green leaves and loose spikes up to one ft (30cm) long, each bearing many small lavender flowers in May and June. It will grow to 3 or 4ft (90–120cm) high.

Hedera helix, the common ivy, is very well known. It is a very popular and adaptable plant, that will grow in almost any conditions from dense shade to full sunlight and in any type of soil. It also makes good ground cover providing it is kept within bounds. There is a considerable number of varieties ranging from those with white or yellow variagations, and there are also wide variations in the size and shape of the leaves, some being most attractive.

Two other beautiful ivies which should be mentioned are, first, the variegated form of *Hedera canariensis*, the Canary Island ivy, called 'Variegata' or 'Gloire de Marengo'. It is a strong grower with large rounded leaves, green in the centre, but merging into silvery grey irregular markings with a whitish border around the edge. The leaves may be injured in exposed cold windswept localities. The other is the variegated form of *Hedera colchica*, the Persian ivy ('Dentata Variegata'), having thick heart-shaped leaves up to 6in. (15cm) broad and as much long, often green shades in the middle with very conspicuous pale yellow to cream irregular variegations towards the outside of the leaves. This is the most handsome of all the large leaved ivies and is quite hardy.

Hoheria lyallii is a large, deciduous, branching shrub, with heart-shaped leaves and white flowers produced in July. *Hoheria glabrata* is similar in growth and flower but is considered to be hardier, while *H. sexstylosa* is a handsome evergreen which is sometimes defoliated in cold winters, but quickly recovers.

The genus **Holboellia** contains five species of evergreen climbers, of which only one, *H. coriacea*, is hardy in Britain. This species is vigorous, growing up to 20ft (6m) or more, and has twining stems which bear dark green glossy trifoliate leaves. The male flowers, which usually appear in April, are purplish in colour, while the female flowers are greenish white and appear a little later. Both types of flower are borne on the same plant.

The climbing hydrangea, **Hydrangea petiolaris**, will cover a large area, and flower profusely even on a north wall. It is very hardy and will cling closely to walls by means of the aerial roots produced on its stem. It is deciduous with rich green, egg-shaped pointed leaves which have sharply toothed edges and turn a pleasing shade of pale yellow in the autumn. The flattish heads of greenish white flowers are edged with conspicuous, white, sterile florets. It is an accommodating plant and will grow successfully in every aspect.

Honeysuckle (see *Lonicera*, p. 106).

An unusual shrub is **Itea ilicifolia**, a native of central China, an evergreen with shiny holly-like leaves. The small greenish white flowers are borne on extremely elegant slender drooping racemes 6 to 9in. (15–20cm) long during August. A young plant over 5ft (1.5m) high and as much across is growing at Kew in a narrow border facing south, sheltered at the back by a wall. It certainly makes an excellent wall plant, but perhaps not so colourful as many other plants (see p. 105).

Ivy (see *Hedera*, opposite).

Probably the best known of the jasmines is **Jasminum officinale**, the common, white, sweetly scented jasmine, which has been cultivated in gardens for so long that the date of its introduction is forgotten. It is a native of Iran and countries eastwards as far as Kashmir and China. It is hardy in the south of England and it lends itself admirably to training up walls and pillars, looking most effective in flower when its long shoots bearing sprays of pure white blossoms are growing through or over other vegetation. It flowers throughout the whole of the summer.

It is a very vigorous grower making shoots sometimes as much as 6ft (1.8m) or more in a single season, but needing support by ties or nails to the wall. With such an amount of growth, it is not surprising that some thinning out of old growth is needed every year or so, otherwise a thicket of tangled stems is formed. Plants can be pruned in early spring, severely if necessary, for it flowers on the current year's growth, or in late summer after flowering.

Jasminum nudiflorum, the yellow winter flowering jasmine, is a deciduous shrub of loose habit growing as much as 10 to 15ft (3–4.5 m) high, but can easily be kept at half that height by pruning. It is quite hardy in the open but when grown with the shelter of a wall comes into flower earlier and is not so likely to be disfigured after severe frosty weather. It is a first rate plant for giving a bright display during mid winter. As it flowers on growth

Above: *Halimium lasianthum* begins flowering in May (see p. 100)
Below: *Eccremocarpus scaber*, a distinctive semi-woody climber (see p. 98)

Above: *Lonicera × brownii*, a decorative and fairly hardy honeysuckle (see p. 107)
Below: *Itea ilicifolia*, a valuable evergreen shrub (see p. 103)

made the previous season, any pruning – such as cutting out old or redundant growth – should be done in spring after the flowering season is finished.

Kerria japonica 'Pleniflora' is a deciduous shrub which is quite hardy and will grow to about 10ft (2.4m). Its growth is rather lanky and it needs artificial support; wires or trellis are suitable. Double yellow flowers are borne in profusion from April to June. Kerrias are easily increased by cuttings.

Lathyrus latifolius, the everlasting pea, is a hardy perennial that appreciates a good, rich soil. It blooms during July and August and the flowers vary in colour from purple and pink to white. Train it up wire netting or trellis, and water frequently in dry spells. Propagation is by seed sown in the spring or by root or shoot cuttings taken in April.

Members of the **Lonicera** (honeysuckle) family are valued chiefly for their fragrant flowers; there are both climbers and shrubs amongst the genus, and all like a good loamy soil with plenty of moisture to keep their roots cool. Nearly all prefer semi-shade, where the flowering parts of the plant are in sunlight, conditions similar to those required by the clematis. They require little annual pruning except for an occasional thinning of old or weak growth and tying in all new growth wherever possible.

Several species are well worth including; *Lonicera × americana* is an extremely vigorous and free flowering plant, which grows to a height of 18 to 20ft (5.4–6.2m). The flowers are fragrant, opening white but gradually ageing to deep yellow with a tinge of purple on the outside of each flower. It is a first-class plant, flowering in June and July.

Lonicera japonica 'Halliana' is a vigorous twiner which is more or less evergreen, and if well grown can make a show during June and July with very fragrant flowers of pure white becoming yellow with maturity.

Our native honeysuckle, *Lonicera periclymenum*, often seen scrambling over the hedgerows in the countryside, is well worth including if space permits. The flowers are fragrant, whitish yellow suffused with purple, produced in close whorls at the end of the twining shoots from June till August and sometimes later. The form 'Serotina' is later in flowering, from July to October, with a similar type of growth and flowers reddish purple outside, creamy white changing to yellow on the inside.

Lonicera sempervirens, the trumpet honeysuckle, is a very beautiful species from the United States, but unfortunately it is a plant which only does really well in milder parts of the country. From June until the autumn its whorls of bright orange-scarlet blossoms are offset well above the glaucous green oval leaves.

In colder gardens where *L. sempervirens* does not grow successfully one can try *L.* × *brownii*. This is a hybrid between *L. sempervirens* and *L. hirsuta*, a semi-evergreen twiner of moderate growth, producing orange-scarlet flowers during the summer months. It is a good wall plant which has inherited much of the beauty of *L. sempervirens* and the hardiness of *L. hirsuta* (see p. 105).

Lonicera tragophylla, a vigorous deciduous honeysuckle from central China, has large flowers, of probably the brightest yellow to be seen in honeysuckles; they are borne in large clusters of ten to twenty during June and July, and contrast well with the oval glaucous green leaves. One great disappointment of this lovely plant is that it has no fragrance. It is perfectly hardy and appears to thrive best in southern England if planted in semi-shade.

No selection would be complete without *L. etrusca*, a very fine Mediterranean species which requires the protection of a south wall if it is to be seen at its best. It has the same type of growth as the common species, but is freer and more vigorous; the very fragrant flowers, yellow, tinged with red, begin to open in July and go on flowering until the autumn on the current season's growth.

The genus **Magnolia** provides some of the most handsome of all flowering trees. Although the majority are perfectly hardy and grow well in the open ground, there are a number well suited for wall cultivation providing the soil is well drained and enriched with plenty of peat and well decayed leafmould, or other forms of compost at the time of planting.

Magnolia denudata – known as the Yulan – was introduced into this country from China in 1788, and has proved to be one of the most beautiful and distinctive of all the magnolias having large, glistening white, well-shaped flowers displayed in early spring. Unfortunately in some seasons the blooms can be damaged by frost, which is the reason why it is often grown in the shelter of a south or west-facing wall.

One of the most popular and widely grown is *Magnolia* × *soulangeana* (which has *M. denudata* as one of its parents and which it closely resembles in its low spreading habit of growth) with flowers varying in different shades of mauve on the outside of the petals (see p. 108).

There are several forms of this hybrid (*M. denudata* and *M. liliiflora*) in cultivation, all varying in colour and shape of flowers, but one of the best with white fragrant flowers is *Magnolia* × *soulangeana* 'Alba Superba'. This is sometimes known as 'Alba', a name also applied to a similar form of *M.* × *soulangeana*, 'Amabilis'. But one of my favourites is *Magnolia* × *soulangeana* 'Rustica Rubra', another fine form with large globular rosy purple flowers often

Above: *Magnolia × soulangeana*, one of the best known members of this handsome genus (see p. 107)
Below: *Rosa* 'Mme Grégoire Staechelin', a climber flowering in early summer (see p. 115)

Above: *Piptanthus laburnifolius*, an evergreen shrub suitable for a wall
(see p. 110)
Below: *Solanum crispum* 'Glasnevin', a vigorous, loose-spreading
rambler (see p. 117)

flowering just as the leaves are about to unfold.

Magnolia stellata, a native of Japan, a much branched shrub with a compact habit of growth, makes another useful plant. The highly scented white, star-shaped flowers are freely produced in March and April, but as it flowers so early in the year the delicate flowers are liable to frost damage. For the small garden and wall cultivation this is a most desirable species.

Magnolia grandiflora is probably the most handsome of all the evergreen species in cultivation; it was introduced from the southern United States to this country in the early 18th century, and makes a very fine tree. Many large specimens are to be seen growing in some of the very large private or public gardens, but it does need a lot of space to develop to the full and must be well secured to the wall by strong wires, hooks or other means of support against strong winds.

The leathery large leaves are dark glossy green, covered beneath with thick red brown felt particularly when young, and the very fine creamy white, bowl-shaped flowers are large and fragrant, continually produced during the late summer and autumn. There are named seedling forms in cultivation each of which claim to be better than the type, more compact in growth, or either having larger flowers or some slight variation in leaf shape.

Myrtus communis, the common myrtle, is not hardy enough to grow in the open in most districts, but it does make a neat and pleasing evergreen shrub for covering a wall with its brilliant dark leaves contrasting with the large white rounded flowers, in the centre of which are conspicuous clusters of numerous stamens. The flowers are usually solitary on slender stalks about 1in. (2.5cm) long arising from the leaf axils in July and August.

Osmanthus delavayi. This charming evergreen shrub was introduced from western China in 1890 and is ideal for wall cultivation, because although it is hardy in the open at Kew and other parts of southern England and the west, the flowers are often damaged by late spring frosts. The plant is relatively slow growing with a spreading bushy habit eventually reaching a height of 6ft (1.8m) or more. It has small leathery dark green glossy leaves and clusters of small pure white funnel-shaped flowers which are very fragrant. These are produced in the axils of the leaves on growth made the previous season, therefore any pruning required should be done immediately after the flowering season.

Parthenocissus: *Parthenocissus henryana* is hardy and quick growing with attractive dark purplish green, deeply lobed leaves, which are beautifully marked by pink and white midribs and veins. In addition it is self-clinging and the leaves, which have more pronounced markings when the plant is grown in shade, turn shades of red in the autumn. *Parthenocissus tricuspidata*, a species from China, Korea and Japan, is well known for forming a dense cover on old town walls and for its brilliant autumn colour, as well as for its incorrect name of Virginia creeper. The true Virginia creeper is in fact *P. quinquefolia* from eastern U.S.A. Its leaves are usually composed of five oval stalked leaflets which are glaucescent beneath, while those of *P. tricuspidata* are broadly egg-shaped and three lobed. Both are self-clinging, turn colour richly in autumn and are valuable for covering high walls (see p. 68).

Few of the passion flowers are suited for growing outdoors except in the more favoured parts of Britain, but I have seen several good specimens of the blue passion flower **Passiflora caerulea** growing successfully in the south on a warm sheltered wall. Given these conditions and a well drained soil, plants will quite often come through a mild winter, although they may suffer during a severe one, which is to be expected being a native of southern Brazil. But for anyone who is prepared to take a risk it can be a most rewarding plant. As a precaution the lower 3 to 4 ft (90–120cm) of stem should be given some protective covering against possible frosty weather.

It is a vigorous climber which will cover quite a large area of space in a growing season, supporting itself by means of tendrils produced at the ends of the leaves. It does sometimes need extra support, such as the use of strong bamboo stakes and tying material, particularly when young plants are being trained. The flowers are borne freely on long stalks on the current year's growth, and are large pale greenish blue in colour, often 4in. (10 cm) across, with that remarkable fascinating centre which is characteristic of this well-known flower (see p. 112).

Pilostegia viburnoides (often known as *Schizophragma viburnoides*), a Chinese evergreen climber which will grow up to 10ft (3m) or more, is another very useful self-clinging plant which climbs by means of aerial roots. The dull green leathery leaves contrast well with the white terminal panicles of flower in late summer, and it is the conspicuous stamens which make the inflorescence so attractive. A good specimen which flowers profusely every year is to be seen at Kew growing on a south wall.

The Himalayan **Piptanthus laburnifolius** (syn. *P. nepalensis*), sometimes called the evergreen laburnum, is a first-class plant for a wall not only because it is an attractive shrub but also because it is not generally hardy. It will reach a height of 6 to 7ft (1.8–2.1 m) and has strong, upright, green woody shoots. These carry glossy trifoliolate leaves, grey beneath, and in late spring they

Above: *Vitis coignetiae*, a very strong-growing vine with large and ornamental foliage, which turns colour in autumn (see p. 119)
Below: The passion flower, *Passiflora caerulea*, is well worth trying outside (see p. 111)

Above: *Wisteria sinensis* is the species widely grown, often reaching a great age (see p. 119)
Below: *Ribes speciosum* bears striking fuchsia-like flowers (see p. 114)

carry erect clusters of deep yellow pea-shaped flowers (see p. 109).

Prunus triloba ('Multiplex'; 'Plena') is a beautiful Chinese cherry which although hardy can be seen at its best when trained against a south or west wall. It will reach a height of 10ft (3m) or more, and flowers in great profusion about the end of March or early April with large pink double blossoms. As the flowers are produced on the shoots of the previous summer, these should be pruned back immediately after flowering to about 2 or 3in. (5–7 cm) from the old wood, so encouraging strong new growth from dormant basal buds (see p. 80).

Pyracantha, the fire-thorn, is a very useful group of evergreen plants, all of which have a profusion of small white flowers in June. They are grown chiefly for the freedom with which they produce their berries in autumn, when they look most attractive if neatly trained against a wall or fence, although they are also hardy in an open situation. They need only occasional pruning to keep them within bounds.

Probably the best known is *P. coccinea*, a south European species with clusters of coral-red fruits. Its cultivar 'Orange Glow' is more widely grown, being more vigorous in growth with larger orange berries, which make a wonderful display. *Pyracantha atalantioides* is equally attractive with dark glossy evergreen foliage and scarlet fruits which usually ripen later and remain on the bush much longer than *P. coccinea*. It too is a very strong grower.

Pyracantha rogersiana is a much less robust grower with small, glossy evergreen leaves and fearsome thorns. It bears an abundance of orange berries which remain fresh until February-March, providing the birds do not take them. The cultivar 'Flava' has very lovely bright yellow fruits. Both plants will do well in positions which get little or no sun during the day.

Ribes speciosum. A very decorative deciduous, or partly ever-green, shrub belonging to the gooseberry family. As it is a native of California it prefers a well drained soil and sheltered sunny position, attaining a height of 5 to 6ft (1.5–1.8m) or more in some districts.

The strong spiny shoots and branches are clothed with small glossy roundish leaves not unlike those of a gooseberry, on which hang clusters of bright crimson pendant flowers not unlike tiny fuchsia blooms, which in some seasons produce small bristly red gooseberry-like fruits (see p. 113).

Romneya coulteri, native of California, is another attractive plant which thrives against a warm south-facing wall in well drained soil. It is a semi-shrubby perennial with a fleshy rootstock which makes it difficult to transplant once established. It is best treated as a herbaceous perennial, cutting back the woody shoots to within a few inches of the ground each spring. This encourages strong new shoots 4 to 6ft (1.2–1.8m) high, bearing glaucous blue grey foliage and producing large white poppy-like flowers with conspicuous golden yellow stamens from June until early autumn. Young plants may take a few years to become established. In colder districts some light winter protection around the base of the plants may be advisable.

Most climbing species of **Rosa** are too vigorous to train on walls but are spectacular when growing up and through trees. On the other hand R. *banksiae*, the Banksian rose, which has been in cultivation for almost 200 years, will grow successfully on a south wall. It is evergreen and thornless, and the growths though slender, will grow many feet in a season. It only flowers once a year in May and June. Usually the flowers are of a soft yellow, single or double, but they may be white; the double form, scented of violets, is more easily obtained. 'Mermaid' is a most beautiful plant for walls with sprays of large pale primrose yellow single flowers which start to open in June and carry on to the autumn frosts. It is semi-evergreen and has glossy bronzy green foliage and vicious spines. It is altogether far more vigorous and hardy than R. *bracteata*, the Macartney rose, which is one of its parents.

Other popular and easily available roses that can be grown up walls successfully include 'Albertine', which has salmon-pink flowers and grows up to 15ft (4.6m); 'Golden Showers', with large, golden-yellow blooms, 6–8 ft (1.8–2.4 m); and 'Mme Grégoire Staechelin' which has coral-pink blooms borne from late spring to early summer, 20 ft (6 m). 'Parkdirektor Riggers' is a very free-flowering climber which bears beautiful deep crimson flowers throughout the summer and early autumn and grows to 12–15ft (3.7–4.6 m) while 'Zéphirine Drouhin' has lovely bright pink, fragrant flowers which also flower throughout the summer, 10–15 ft (3–4.6m) (see p. 108). (See also the Wisley Handbook *Roses*.)

There are a number of shrubby late-flowering **salvias** which can be considered for wall planting. *Salvia greggii, S. microphylla* (syn. *S. grahamii*) and its variety *neurepia* are all sub-shrubby Mexican species worth trying at the foot of a warm wall for their brilliant scarlet flowers in late autumn. This can also be said of *Salvia coerulea* (also known as *S. ambigens* and *S. guaranitica*) in which the flowers are deep blue, produced on long terminal racemes. It is a first-class plant 4 to 5ft (1.2–1.5m) tall with shoots dying back in winter, but not absolutely hardy in all areas. Plants will require either some protection over the roots or to be lifted and stored like dahlias in a frost-proof building (see p.116). The genus **Schisandra** is a rather unusual and interesting group

Above: The small shrubby salvias do well at the base of a warm wall (see p. 115)
Below: *Schizophrgma integrifolium* is closely related to hydrangea

of shrubby plants, which make long, vigorous, slender twining shoots each year, on which single pendulous, highly-coloured unisexual flowers are borne in considerable numbers in the leaf axils during April and May. The flowers of S. sphenanthera are bright orange, and of S. rubriflora are deep crimson. In both, the red fruits are borne on stalks some 4 to 6in. (10–15cm) long. Both species eventually reach a height of 10 to 12ft (3–3.6 m). They are not very fastidious as to soil requirements, but seem to succeed best on a sheltered wall partially shaded from the midday sun of summer. I have seen them flowering and growing well on a wall facing north and east.

Schizophragma integrifolium, another magnificent Chinese plant, is a strong growing climbing shrub, having large heart-shaped deciduous leaves 4 to 6in. (10–15cm) long and the same mode of growth as *Pilostegia viburnoides* (see p. 111) to which it is closely allied.

The fertile inconspicuous flowers are surrounded by remarkable sterile flowers consisting of enormous creamy white bracts sometimes as much as 4in. (10cm) long, flowering during July. The plant seems to dislike full sun, particularly in the southern parts of the country.

Where space permits **Solanum** is a worthwhile group of plants, best described as very vigorous ramblers which require some support. First is *Solanum crispum*, introduced from Chile about 1830; when grown at its best it is a most graceful and lovely plant and quite hardy if grown on a south or west wall. It is a very quick grower, more or less evergreen with a loose, spreading habit. On growth made during the current season, the potato-like flowers are produced very freely during June and July, deep lavender in colour with conspicuous yellow stamens in the centre of each flower. The cultivar 'Glasnevin' is the best form to grow on account of its longer season of flower (see p. 109).

The other species S. jasminoides, also an evergreen, is slender and twining in growth and slightly more tender, which is not surprising since it is a native of Brazil. However, it will thrive and flower well if given a warm sheltered position and a well drained soil. It flowers from July to September in great profusion, the individual flowers being pale blue in colour and borne in loose clusters on the current season's growth. There is also a white-flowered variety.

Solanums normally flower on long stalked corymbs on growth made during the current year; any pruning required should therefore be done in spring before new growth starts. The pruning consists of cutting out the old flower heads from the previous year and any very old stems or overcrowded growth.

Apart from this no hard pruning is required. Tie in all new vigorous growth as it develops during the summer.

A highly ornamental and attractive shrub is **Sophora tetraptera**, a native of New Zealand, where it is called Kowhai. It makes a large shrub or small tree in this country, with golden yellow, pea-like flowers carried on pendulous racemes during May and early June. Its pinnate leaves give the whole plant a very light and graceful appearance. A plant growing on the west wall of the Temperate House at Kew has come through severe winters unharmed. It produces plenty of seed especially after a good summer.

Stauntonia hexaphylla is a very strong growing climber, with leathery evergreen leaves composed of up to seven leaflets, and fragrant, violet tinted white flowers.

Another evergreen **Trachelospermum jasminoides** *(Rhyncospermum)* is a delightfully shrubby plant with a twining habit of growth, which eventually reaches a height of 6 to 8ft (1.8–2.4 m), although young plants seem to be slow to make a start. Its pure white, fragrant, jasmine-like flowers are produced in July and August and look very effective against the dark glossy evergreen leaves. It is quite hardy on a south or west wall, and does not need any artificial support.

Virginia creeper (see *Parthenocissus quinquefolia* p. 111).

Vitis, the vine family, includes many species and varieties grown chiefly for their attractive foliage, but also for their fruits. Many are really too vigorous for all but large gardens with ample wall space, but some of those described below can be grown satisfactorily as long as they are restrained (i.e. pruned back and tied regularly).

Vitis 'Brant' is a strong growing hybrid which is sometimes listed under V. *vinifera*, the common grape vine. It has attractive 3 to 5 lobed leaves, which turn to shades of dark red and purple in autumn, and an additional attraction is cylindrical bunches of sweet, aromatic, dark purple grapes with a bloom. Of the common grape vine itself the clone 'Purpurea' has claret-purple leaves which contrast well with silver foliage plants.

Vitis amurensis from Manchuria is moderately strong growing with broad 3 to 5 lobed leaves which colour a wonderful red in autumn.

Vitis coignetiae is exceptionally vigorous with splendid rounded, dark green leaves, which are sometimes as much as 12 in. (30cm) long and 10in. (25cm) broad. Though they often change to various shades of red in the autumn, they give an air of almost tropical luxuriance throughout the growing season. As with most strong growing *Vitis* it is necessary in February or early March of each year to prune back the shoots to 2 or 3 buds at the base of the previous season's growth so as to keep the plant within bounds. Where it is necessary to increase its size to cover more wall space in subsequent years, select a few of the strong growths and prune back to 12 or 18in. (30–45cm) in length, or longer if required, of the previous season's growth (see p. 112).

Winter sweet (see *Chimonanthus praecox* p. 91).

Wisteria is one of the most ornamental deciduous hardy climbers we have for outdoor cultivation. With long hanging racemes of mauve or lilac flowers, it is too familiar a sight to need description. Wisterias are easily cultivated and will grow in any good soil, but a sunny position is essential to get them to flower well, therefore a wall makes an ideal site.

If planted in a restricted area a fair amount of pruning may have to be done each year to keep them within bounds; usually the long annual shoots not required should be shortened back to about 6 in. (15cm) long in early August and these shortened shoots cut back again to within three or four buds during the winter. If left unpruned plants are apt to grow into a thick tangle of inter- twining stems, which generally do not flower, for the best sprays are produced from buds formed towards the base of the current season's growth. They can also damage drainpipes and guttering if allowed to get out of control. In young plants, however, a certain amount of this whippy growth must be retained when a young plant is being trained into position. For the first two or three years after planting a young plant may only produce a limited amount of new growth; this is to be expected until a greater root system has been built up, after which the annual growth will increase considerably.

Wisteria sinensis (W. chinensis) is the species commonly grown and many fine old specimens are to be seen, some of which have been grown in this country for well over a hundred years. It is a very vigorous grower and if correctly trained in its young state will cover a large wall space and flower freely in May. Quite often a second but much smaller crop of flowers is produced during August on the current year's growth (see p. 113).

There is also a white flowered form 'Alba' which forms an effective contrast when grown with the type.

A less common species is *Wisteria venusta*, which is not such a strong grower. It is similar to *W. sinensis* but the flowers are larger and are a lovely pure white with a yellow tinge at the base of each flower, and delicately fragrant. It comes into bloom after *W. sinensis* has finished.

Above: *Lathyrus odoratus*, the popular annual sweet pea (see p. 123)
Below left: *Rhodochiton volubile*, a Mexican climber which flowers
profusely throughout the summer and autumn (see p. 124)
Below right: *Tropaeolum peregrinum*, the canary creeper, easily raised
from seed (see p. 125)

Annual Climbing Plants

There are quite a number of annual climbing plants which can be successfully grown in association with the more permanent plants, particularly on parts of the wall which are not already clothed. They can also be used for filling up other gaps where the stems of some of the taller and stronger growing plants have become bare at the base (the rose 'Mermaid' has this tendency), thus providing a means of support up which the annuals can climb and eventually becoming attached through the upper branches by the time they reach flowering stage.

The extra shelter and protection, particularly along a south or west-facing wall, provide good growing conditions for some of the half-hardy annuals which are often grown in cool greenhouse conditions.

Seed should be sown in a well-drained potting compost or seed compost during April and early May and placed in a little heat (50–55°F, 10–13°C) to hasten germination. If no heat is available plants can be successfully raised using a cold frame, or even cloches.

When the seedlings are large enough prick them out, either singly, or three to a 3½in. (9cm) size pot, according to their vigour. Once established the seedlings can be transferred to a cold frame for hardening off, eventually planting them into their flowering position with the least possible root disturbance. A few short twigs, pea sticks or similar material placed around the young plants to give them support can be advantageous at planting time.

Some of the more tender types of annuals should not be sown until the middle of May when growing conditions are warmer and the chances of late frosts have disappeared.

It is possible to sow the hardier types direct into the positions where they are to flower; if this is done care should be taken not to sow too thickly. When the seedlings are large enough to handle, thin out to 3 or 4in. (7–10cm) apart, or even more, according to their vigour.

In some of the larger well-stocked garden centres some of these plants can be found already established in pots or containers ready for planting at the appropriate time of the season.

Blumenbachia lateritia. This curious Chilean plant has also been known as *Caiophora laterita* and *Loasa laterita*. The stems

121

have a twining habit of growth, up to 4 to 5ft (1.2–1.5m) in height, having divided pinnate or deeply lobed leaves. Single bright orange-red flowers are borne on long twisting stalks which enable the plant to support itself. *Blumenbachia* flowers well into the autumn, and as the long narrow fruits develop they take on a very unusual spiral or twisting effect.

Both the stem and leaves are covered with stinging hairs, making the plant very difficult to handle and necessitating the use of gloves. It is best treated as a half hardy annual, seed being sown singly in pots in spring, preferably in a little heat, and grown on. After hardening off the seedlings should be transferred to their permanent flowering position in early May in a warm sheltered position, allowing 6 to 8in. (15–20cm) between each plant.

Canary creeper (see *Tropaeolum peregrinum*, p. 125).

Cardiospermum halicacabum, commonly called the balloon vine or heart-pea, originates from the tropics and is a very interesting rapid-growing, climbing annual up to 6ft (1.8m) tall which is able to support itself by tendrils.

The slender, pointed and deeply-toothed light green foliage creates a very feathery appearance from which arise clusters of small white flowers, followed by large green ornamental inflated seed pods containing seeds which have medicinal properties. It is for these attractive fruits that the plant is grown.

Cobaea scandens, also known as the cup and saucer flower, is a native of Central and South America. This strong growing climber will reach a height of 15ft (4.5m) or more, and has angular branching stems which bear oval-shaped leaflets, sometimes with tendrils attached; the large bell-shaped solitary flowers are violet on the outside and greenish white on the inside, and are produced in succession from July to October.

Although best suited for a cool greenhouse it will thrive in a warm sheltered position on a south or west-facing wall, but is best treated as an annual and raised each year from seed sown in early spring in a little heat.

Cucumis anguria is a slender climbing annual from the American tropics. When grown on a wall, this plant will reach a height of 6 to 8ft (1.8–2.4m) bearing small lobed leaves and solitary flowers from which are produced attractive gooseberry-like gourds during the summer and autumn. *Cucumis* is best raised from seed in early May with the aid of a little heat, similar to the requirements of marrows and cucumbers to which it is closely allied.

Cucurbita pepo is a very variable species which botanically covers a wide variety of ornamental grounds, pumpkins, and marrows of various shapes, sizes and colouring when in fruit (which is the feature for which they are prized). They are very vigorous in growth with large dark green leaves, some palmate, lobed or roundish in shape, and they need support and tying up during the height of its growing season. Cucurbita is best raised from seed in late spring, and given the same cultural conditions as the garden marrow, with plenty of water during the dry summer periods.

Humulus japonicus var. **lutescens** is an interesting, vigorous Japanese climber, grown mainly for its large palmate-shaped leaves which are gold or bronze yellow in colour. This species can be grown from seed and treated as an annual, although there is also a variegated form having green-gold leaves which can be just as attractive but does not always come true from seed; the true variegated plant must be raised from cuttings.

Ipomoea purpurea (morning glory), is a very handsome twiner, growing 6 to 8ft (1.8–2.4m) in height when grown in the open. It bears cordate-shaped leaves and large exquisite sky-blue flowers from June to September. The flowers are short-lived, being fully open in the morning and closing as the day advances, but the beauty of this plant is that there is always a succession of buds to open during the height of its flowering season.

Lagenaria siceraria (bottle gourd) is from another genus closely allied to Cucurbita with similar heart-shaped leaves and tendrils by which it can support its stems. The white, starlike flowers are borne in clusters, and these develop into large, yellow, bottle-shaped fruits. Although usually grown in a warm greenhouse it is hardy enough for cultivation as a summer annual.

Lathyrus odoratus (sweet pea). This very well known and popular annual, noted for its delightful fragrance, makes a useful and easy growing plant, particularly for use on areas of wall where the more permanent plants are still small and have yet to fill their allotted space. It does however need some means of support such as wires, canes or pea sticks to which the tendrils can attach themselves (see p. 120).

There are a large number of cultivars and colours available, but I shall not name them here as any good seed catalogue can be consulted for up-to-date varieties.

To get really good quality, sweet peas should be sown in late autumn (September) preferably one or two seeds in a $3\frac{1}{2}$in. (9cm) pot or up to 12 seeds in a 6in. (15cm) pot, in seed or potting compost and overwintered in a cold frame. An alternative is to sow in early spring in similar conditions, or better still with a little heat to hasten germination; harden off before planting out into their flowering position. Growing plants benefit by regular feeding when the buds start to develop.

Maurandya barclaiana, a showy, delicate climber, can climb by the twisting of the leafstalk around any form of support it contacts. This plant often becomes woody at the base and has leaves more or less triangular in shape, toothed and covered with fine downy hairs. The flowers are tubular in shape, not unlike those of a foxglove, usually solitary and produced in the leaf axils. They are violet purple on the outside with a greenish tinge on the inside.

Maurandya erubescens, another species similar in growth and appearance but with rose-pink coloured flowers and whitish tube, is an ideal tender plant for growing outside during the summer months against a sheltered warm south or west facing wall. Sow the seed in early spring in a warm greenhouse, and do not plant outdoors until May or early June when all signs of late frosts have vanished. Both species are now included in the genus *Asarina*.

Nasturtium (see *Tropaeolum majus* opposite).

Quamoclit coccinea (star ipomoea). A charming little annual twining herb growing 3 to 4ft (0.9–1.2m) and sometimes higher, is ideal for a warm sheltered pocket, and has slender, pointed, sword-like leaves from the axils of which grow tubular-shaped flowers 1 to 1½in. (2–3cm) in length, scarlet on the outside with yellow in the throat.

Quamoclit lobata is sometimes known as *Mina lobata* or *Ipomoea versicolor*. Another vigorous twining plant similar in habit to the previous species, it grows to a height of 4 to 5ft (1.2–1.5 m) and sometimes taller in a hot summer, having small lobed leaves, and clusters of tubular flowers which are bright crimson turning to orange and then yellow with age. It flowers from June to September.

Quamoclit pennata (Cyprus vine) is sometimes grown under the name *Ipomoea quamoclit*, and is another species with similar slender twining habit which grows to the same height as the previous species. It has fine pinnate leaves and scarlet, funnel-shaped flowers from June to September. A variety with white flowers is also known and ocasionally seen in cultivation.

All the species of *Quamoclit* are best treated as half hardy annuals, and can be raised from seed sown in a little heat if available, alternatively they may be sown in the open where they are to flower in May. They are now included in the genus *Ipomoea*.

Rhodochiton volubile, sometimes called *R. atrosanguineum*, is an extremely beautiful and free flowering Mexican climber, which can be successfully grown out of doors if given a warm, sheltered south facing situation, where the stems can twine to effect among other small foliage plants (see p. 120).

The leaves are cordate in shape, being somewhat slender and pointed with long twisting leaf stalks which help it to climb. The curious dark blood-red, almost black, parasol-shaped flowers look very effective with the wide saucer shaped rose-pink calyx.

Sow the seed in March or early April preferably in a little heat, and harden off before planting out. It will give a long season of flower starting from June until late autumn.

Sweet pea (see *Lathyrus odoratus* p. 123).

Thunbergia alata (commonly called blackeyed Susan). This plant, a native of South Africa, has become very popular for growing outside during the summer months.

It is a soft hairy twining annual, growing to a height of 5ft (1.5 m) or more during a hot season, with ovate to cordate-shaped leaves and decorative flowers of rich orange with a distinct blackish-brown centre surrounded by two large inflated bracts. Other coloured forms are in cultivation, varying from white through to shades of yellow.

Trichosanthes anguina (serpent or snake gourd). This is a tall, slender, twining annual with soft, downy stems, roundish leaves, and fragrant clusters of white fringed flowers which develop into very long fruits, sometimes twisted, with green and white stripes when young but turning to a bright orange when ripe. This gourd requires similar conditions to *Cucumis* (p. 122).

Tropaeolum peregrinum (*T. aduncum*) is commonly called canary creeper. This is one of the most attractive climbing annuals within the genus (see p. 120).

The soft green stems will grow up to 6 to 8ft (1.8–2.4m) high, bearing deeply-cut, lobed glaucous green leaves which make a fine contrast to the fringed lemon-yellow spurred flowers, each arranged on long stalks giving a long season of bloom throughout the summer; a most rewarding plant.

Seed should be sown in April and early May, singly in small pots or 3 seeds in a $3\frac{1}{2}$in. (9cm) size pot, germinated in a cold frame and planted out to the flowering position when large enough. Seed may also be sown direct into the flowering position in a well drained but not too rich soil.

Requiring similar cultivation is the ever popular garden nasturtium **Tropaeolum majus**, a vigorous annual, which has roundish glabrous green leaves. The large usually orange (although other colours are obtainable) flowers continue throughout the summer months and well into the autumn. The nasturtium is one of the easiest annuals to grow and will flourish on a poor, dry soil. If it is to be treated as a climber some means of support is required, but it can also be left to trail along the ground where it will grow and flower quite successfully.

Above: A plum tree trained against a wall
Below: Peach 'Peregrine' fruits in early August

Wall-trained Fruit

Fruits are another group of plants which enjoy the shelter of a wall if space is available; they include apples, pears, plums (including gages), peaches, apricots and nectarines, and all provide, in addition to good quality fruit, a display of flower in the spring. Apples are the least likely to need the shelter of a wall, but the others benefit from the extra warmth which will improve the flavour of the fruits.

Good examples of trained fruit trees can still occasionally be seen on kitchen garden walls in some of the large private gardens, all beautifully pruned and trained with not a shoot out of place, the results of many years of work from the skilled gardener. Nowadays, with smaller gardens, they are sometimes trained on a suitable house or boundary wall.

Normally all these different types of fruits, with perhaps the exception of peaches, nectarines and apricots, are also successful in the open ground, but growing them on a wall does afford some protection from late spring frosts when the trees are in flower; this particularly applies to plums and gages. It is considered that some of the finest flavoured dessert plums and gages are produced from trees grown against a warm south or west-facing wall.

It is very important to purchase young trees from a reputable fruit grower or a good garden centre, and to make sure that they are healthy and growing on the appropriate rootstock. Work at research stations has produced dwarfing rootstocks which are particularly suitable for using in a small space and these are generally the best choice for growing against a wall. The various methods of training, such as cordon, espalier, or fan (see p. 74) give trees which make maximum use of the space available. They may be purchased as "maidens" (i.e. one year old plants) by the experienced grower and then pruned and trained in accordance with the form of tree he wishes to grow. These are cheaper to buy and usually grow away better than older trees, but for the beginner it is probably better to buy trees up to three or more years old which have already been shaped by the nurseryman.

Planting can be done at any time between November and March providing the weather is fine and the ground not frozen; make sure that the trees have a good root system with plenty of fibrous roots attached. Many garden centres now have fruit trees established in containers which enable planting to be carried out at more or less any time of the year with the least possible disturbance of the root ball.

In all cases fruit trees that are to be grown against a wall prefer a fertile and well-drained soil that has been well dug and prepared before planting as the trees are to remain in that one position for many years to come; this particularly applies to apples and pears. On poor sandy or acid soil, well decayed manure or compost should be incorporated with the addition of a moderate amount of old mortar rubble or some other form of lime; this is particularly beneficial to plums, gages and other stone fruits.

All fruits require plenty of light and moisture during the growing season, and ample space to grow and develop, so the correct distance between trees should be ascertained before planting. It is also wise to avoid planting too close to large surface rooting trees such as elm and poplar, which can soon become a nuisance and impoverish the soil within the borders adjoining the wall.

Once the young trees have been planted, staking and wiring the wall (see p. 72) will be necessary to keep the tree firmly in position, and for tying in the new growth as it develops.

Where ample wall space is available the common fig (*Ficus carica*) is worth growing, chiefly for its fruit, although its handsome ornamental foliage is also most attractive during the summer months. Figs require plenty of sun and warmth and therefore prefer a south-facing wall. It is generally accepted that ripe fruits are more often obtained from trees which are grown in the warmer areas such as the south and west of England, conditions further north of the country being generally too cold for success. One of the most popular and reliable varieties to grow is 'Brown Turkey'.

Figs are generally fan trained (see p. 74) to obtain the best results, tying in new healthy growth when necessary during the growing season. The roots should be confined to a restricted area in order to encourage fruit production, so the fig can be grown in a narrow border.

Winter pruning consists mainly of cutting out all diseased or frost damaged wood and other weak growth which crosses the main branches; this should be done during late March when the severe winter weather has passed.

For further detailed information on cultural instructions and requirements regarding the growing and training of fruit trees on walls, see the well illustrated and comprehensive book entitled *The Fruit Garden Displayed* published by Cassell for the Royal Horticultural Society.

SOME RECOMMENDED VARIETIES:

Apples

Dessert (eating)
      Beauty of Bath (August)
      Egremont Russet (October–November)
      Epicure (August–September)
      James Grieve (September–October)
      Laxton's Fortune (September–October)
      Ellison's Orange (September–November)
      Sunset (November–December)
      Cox's Orange Pippin (November–January)
      Tydeman's Late Orange (April–February)

Pears

Dessert
      Williams Bon Chrétien (September)
      Louise Bonne of Jersey (October)
      Beurré Superfin (October)
      Beurré Hardy (October)
      Doyenné du Comice (November)
      Conference (October–November)

Plums

Dessert and culinary
      Victoria (mid August)
      Pershore (late August)
      Warwickshire Drooper (September)
      Marjorie's Seedling (September)

Gages

Dessert
      Cambridge Gage (end of August)
      Denniston's Superb (mid August)
      Oullins Golden Gage (mid August)
      Jefferson (early September)

Apricots

      Moorpark (August)

Nectarines

John Rivers (mid July)
Lord Napier (early August)
Humboldt (mid August)
Pine Apple (early September)

Peaches

Hale's Early (July)
Peregrine (early August)
Rochester (early August)
Royal George (end of August)
Bellegarde (early to mid September)

Cherries

Most sweet cherries grow too vigorously to be trained to a limited space on a back garden wall. There is not yet a dwarfing rootstock for cherries which would control their growth. Another difficulty with cherries is that at least two different cultivars need to be planted together to get pollination and fruiting. These two problems can be partially overcome by planting a tree of the self-fertile variety 'Stella' on the rootstock 'Colt', which is semi-dwarfing.

Acid cherries, e.g. 'Morello', are suitable for walls as they are self-fertile and relatively small trees which can be easily trained, usually in the fan-form.

Grapes

Vines can also be grown against walls and are very amenable to training. The usual form, however, is a vertical cordon with one or more branches spaced at $3\frac{1}{2}$ to 4ft (1.2m) apart, so allowing space for the fruiting lateral shoots. Among suitable cultivars are:

White

Perle de Czaba (late September)
New York Muscat (mid to end October)
Chasselas (late October)

Black

Noir Hatif de Marseilles (late September)
Cascade (Seibel 13.053) (early October)
Muscat Bleu (mid-October)

(See also the Wisley Handbook, *Grapes Indoors and Out*.)

Soft fruit

Red and white currants and gooseberries can also be grown against walls, with one, two or even three vertical "arms".

Victoria plum has attractive blossoms in the spring and delicious fruit in the autumn

Plants Suitable for Various Aspects

Most wall plants, with the exception of a few that prefer shade and cooler growing conditions, succeed equally well on a wall facing between east, south and west. For preference I would choose a south wall, for it is there that the plants get the benefit of the maximum amount of sunshine. Some prefer a more westerly aspect to get the benefit from the hottest part of the day which can quite often be in the early afternoon during the summer. For plants that bloom in early spring, an east facing wall is less satisfactory. Many flowers will survive a few degrees of frost without injury provided they can thaw out slowly, but if a late frost is followed by bright early morning sunshine, the same flowers receiving a quick thaw can be spoilt. For these plants it may be advantageous to plant them on a south-west to west facing wall. There are, however, many plants that will thrive on walls exposed to the east and south-east, although some discretion may be used in selecting those plants that bloom after March or early April which would miss the late spring frosts. Walls facing north are least satisfactory of all and comparatively few climbers or shrubs prefer them; it is generally evergreens that do best. Even so some shelter from north and north-east winds by other vegetation or buildings is advantageous. For walls fully exposed to these winds especially in cold districts it is difficult to find interesting plants.

A SELECTION FOR NORTH AND EAST WALLS

Camellia japonica cultivars*	Hydrangea petiolaris
Celastrus orbiculatus	Jasminium officinale
Chaenomeles	Lonicera tragophylla
Clematis × jackmanii cultivars	Parthenocissus henryana
Cotoneaster	Parthenocissus quinquefolia
Euonymus fortunei	Pyracantha
Forsythia	Schisandra
Hedera helix and cultivars	Schizophragma integrifolium
Holboellia coriacea	

Most if not all of those items which are listed on a north and east wall will grow also on a south or west wall.

* Except in Scotland and the north of England.

132

A SELECTION FOR A WEST WALL

Abelia floribunda
Actinidia kolomikta
Camellia sasanqua
Camellia saluenensis
Camellia × williamsii cultivars
Ceanothus
Chaenomeles
Chimonanthus praecox
Choisya ternata
Clematis × jackmanii cultivars
Cytisus battandieri
Escallonia

Hoheria lyallii
Jasminum nudiflorum
Lonicera
Magnolia denudata
Osmanthus delavayi
Passiflora caerulea
Pilostegia viburnoides
Prunus triloba
Rosa
Solanum crispum
Solanum jasminoides 'Album'
Wisteria sinensis

A SELECTION FOR A SOUTH WALL

Abelia floribunda
Abutilon megapotamicum
Camellia sasanqua
Camellia saluenensis
Camellia × williamsii cultivars
Campsis
Ceanothus
Chaenomeles
Choisya ternata
Cistus
Clematis
Cytisus battandieri

Desfontainea spinosa
Escallonia
Lonicera japonica 'Halliana'
Magnolia denudata
Osmanthus delavayi
Prunus triloba
Passiflora caerulea
Pilostegia viburnoides
Solanum crispum
Sophora tetraptera
Teucrium fruticans
Wisteria sinensis

Desfontainea spinosa appreciates the shelter of a wall (see p.98)

Growing Dwarf Bulbs

JACK ELLIOTT

Crocuses are ideal for a small, sunny rock garden, flowering
either in the autumn or winter-spring

Introduction

Few plants give better value in the garden than dwarf bulbs. They make up for their small size by their freedom of flowering and ease of cultivation, needing the minimum of attention after planting and increasing happily if left undisturbed. There is a vast range of dwarf bulbs, most of them readily obtainable and inexpensive, and they are suitable for every position from moist shade to hot dry situations. By choosing some of the less well-known ones, the bulb season, which is generally concentrated in March and April, can be extended throughout the year, including the difficult months of late autumn and winter.

This book describes a selection of the most rewarding dwarf bulbs, both the familiar and the more unusual, and gives guidance on their cultivation. Individual chapters are devoted to the major genera – crocus, colchicum, galanthus, leucojum, iris, narcissus, tulip – followed by chapters on other bulbs grouped according to their season of flowering, from autumn to summer.

The term bulb has been used here to embrace not only true bulbs, but corms (e.g. crocus) and tubers (e.g. anemone) which are commonly thought of as "bulbs" and behave in a similar way. However, definitely rhizomatous plants (e.g. certain irises) have been excluded. Height limits have not been applied too strictly, but the majority of plants will be under 12 in. (30 cm) tall and all are hardy in the south of England. A few suggestions are also made for growing them under glass, in an unheated greenhouse or frame, where some of the choicer bulbs can benefit from perfect conditions. All the plants mentioned should be available from trade sources and especially from the numerous bulb specialists who advertise in the gardening press.

Opposite: *Allium murrayanum* is an easily grown onion which flowers in summer

The majority of bulbs are offered for sale in a dry semi-dormant state in the autumn. These should be planted as early as possible, at a depth depending on the size of the bulb and the type of soil, from about 3 in. (8 cm) for the smaller ones to 8 in. (20 cm) for the larger. The importance of good drainage is stressed later (see p. 140) and in heavy soil it is helpful to put coarse sand round the bulbs when planting them. In a few cases, notably cyclamen and snowdrops, the bulbs are usually sold in growth, packed in peat or other moist material, and should be planted immediately. If the ground is frozen, it is advisable to keep them temporarily in pots until conditions have improved. Other summer- and autumn-flowering bulbs may be obtainable in spring or summer and should always be planted as soon as possible.

Most bulbs need only the minimum of care to ensure their survival from year to year and can be left undisturbed after planting. However, some, such as daffodils, will increase so freely that they become overcrowded within about three years, resulting in loss of vigour and fewer flowers. The bulbs should then be lifted during the dormant period, preferably in August or early September, divided and replanted individually in new positions. If they are replaced in the same soil, a general fertilizer such as bonemeal should be incorporated.

As with other garden plants, the first essential for success is a well-prepared soil with adequate nutrients. Bonemeal is an excellent fertilizer, dug in at the time of initial planting, or forked into the surface of the soil as a subsequent top dressing before the bulbs are due to appear. Freshly manured ground should be avoided and must be left at least six months before bulbs are planted.

WHERE TO GROW DWARF BULBS

In grass

Large bold daffodils look their best when growing naturally in rough grass; but anyone who has seen the sheets of *Narcissus bulbocodium* in the alpine meadow at the RHS Garden, Wisley, or at the Savill Garden, Windsor Great Park, will appreciate that their smaller relatives can also be used in this way. Unfortunately,

The native snake's head, *Fritillaria meleagris*, establishes itself happily in grass and increases from seed

the number of dwarf bulbs which can cope with the competition of grass is limited mainly to the more vigorous ones. Among them are *Narcissus bulbocodium*, *N. cyclamineus* and their cultivars, *Scilla bifolia*, Dutch crocuses, *Crocus chrysanthus* hybrids, *C. tommasinianus*, *Fritillaria meleagris*, *F. pyrenaica* and grape hyacinths (*Muscari*) in the spring; *Leucojum aestivum* in the summer; and *Crocus speciosus*, *C. kotschyanus*, *Colchicum autumnale* and *C. speciosum* in the autumn.

It is essential to plant the bulbs at least twice their own depth and to leave the grass uncut until their leaves have started to die down. There are various planting methods. A long-handled bulb planter, designed to be pressed down with the foot, is ideal for the larger bulbs (and much better than the hand-held instrument, which requires considerable pressure and is almost unusable unless the ground is very soft). For small bulbs, sections of turf can be lifted with a spade and the underlying soil loosened, the bulbs planted and the turf replaced; alternatively, a garden fork with broad tines can be used, pushing it into the ground and moving it backwards and forwards to widen the holes, planting the bulbs one to each hole and finally covering with a little loose soil. Care must be taken with this method to vary the position and

139

direction of the fork, so that the bulbs do not appear to be in straight lines: an effect of informal drifts should always be the aim. Planting should be done as soon as the bulbs are available, although it is easier after a period of wet weather. It is also a good idea to cut the grass just before planting.

Bulbs in grass will benefit from occasional top dressings of a general fertilizer, such as Growmore, in February. However, the most important factor in ensuring their continued vigour is to let their leaves die down before cutting the grass. This will be several weeks after they have finished flowering and they will look very untidy. The grass can usually be cut in June, when most of the spring-flowering bulbs will be over, and repeated once or twice before the autumn-flowering crocuses and colchicums come into growth. If you are also hoping for increase from self-sowing, for example, from *Fritillaria meleagris* or *Narcissus bulbocodium*, then the grass cutting must be delayed even longer, until the seed capsules have emptied, frequently two or three weeks after the leaves have died down.

In raised beds or a rock garden

Most bulbs will benefit from the same soil preparation as alpine plants, good drainage being the vital ingredient for both. This can be achieved by raising the bed a little above the surrounding ground and incorporating plenty of horticultural grit in the soil. Although not essential, a top dressing of the same grit helps to conserve moisture and prevent small plants from being battered by heavy rain. (For further information about raised beds, see the Wisley Handbook, *Alpines the Easy Way*.)

A raised bed can accommodate a wide range of dwarf bulbs and alpines, which are small enough to be in scale with each other, whereas bulbs are often lost among larger perennials and shrubs, unless kept well to the front of a border. The alpine plants can also help to prolong the display. Wherever bulbs are grown, however, the question arises of how to fill the bare patches when they are dormant in summer. It is often recommended that they should be planted under low carpeting plants and the rock garden is the best place to try this, using such ground-covering plants as thymes, raoulias and some of the smaller campanulas and phlox. Although in theory this makes maximum use of the space available, it presents problems because many of these plants root as they run, so that the bulbs face severe competition. In addition, the dying foliage of more vigorous bulbs can detract from the overall appearance. Perhaps the best compromise is to place the bulbs in groups between plants which spread widely from a

Osteospermums can be recommended for planting with bulbs, to follow on after these have finished

central rootstock during the growing season and then die back, or can be cut back, for the winter – for instance, the hardier osteospermums, *O. jucundum (Dimorphotheca barberiae)* 'Compacta' and *O. ecklonis* 'Prostrata', *Convolvulus sabatius* and *Sphaeralcea munroana*. Alternatively, the bulbs can be planted between rock garden shrubs which make most of their growth after the bulbs have flowered, such as *Zauschneria californica*, *Ceratostigma willmottianum* and the smaller potentillas.

In borders and flower beds

Much of what has been said about the rock garden applies on a larger scale to planting in beds and borders, especially if the soil is light and well-drained. Most bulbs favour a sunny position and are therefore best planted near the front of a border, where they will not be shaded too heavily by other plants, at least during the growing and flowering season, and where they can also be seen. After the bulbs have died down, partial shade will have little effect on their growth. In fact, all but the most ardent sun-lovers may be planted in the dappled shade of deciduous shrubs and small trees and will appreciate the drier conditions maintained by the tree and shrub roots in summer, as well as the lack of disturbance to the soil.

In a herbaceous border which is regularly cultivated, bulbs may be less successful and can even be a nuisance. However, groups of the more vigorous ones can be planted between herbaceous perennials to advance the flowering season in the earlier part of the year. Many tender perennials have gained popularity recently, because they will grow rapidly from cuttings overwintered under glass – for example, the osteospermums already mentioned and other *Osteospermum* species and hybrids, gazanias and verbenas. These are ideal for associating with bulbs, since they can be cut back in the autumn, after which they may survive the winter. Annuals and bedding plants can be used in a similar way, if one is prepared for the work involved.

Although most rose-growers seem to frown upon any interplanting of roses in formal beds, it is certainly possible to grow dwarf bulbs there, preferably choosing those which are unlikely to need lifting, dividing or other attentions that might disturb the rose roots. Shrub rose enthusiasts will probably have fewer qualms about interplanting, if this can be done before the roses have become too well-established and filled the bed with roots.

In shady situations

A number of bulbs are natives of woodland and will flourish in shady parts of the garden, so long as the soil is enriched with plenty of humus, peat or leaf mould. Most woodland plants also like abundant moisture and these shade-loving bulbs are no exception, although a few of the more vigorous kinds, especially *Cyclamen coum* and *C. hederifolium*, may grow and even increase in dry shade.

Trilliums and erythroniums need moist woodland conditions, which are also enjoyed by many anemones, snowdrops, cyclamen, certain fritillaries and some narcissus. Unfortunately, shade, whether from walls and buildings or from trees and shrubs, often results in poor dry soil and the incorporation of organic matter is essential. The ground close to a wall can be very dry and may require extra watering as well as extra humus. The success of planting under trees, hedges and shrubs depends mainly on the extent of their roots, which deprive smaller plants of both food and moisture. Tall deep-rooting trees like oak provide perfect natural conditions, casting a light shade without impoverishing the surrounding soil. However, many other trees and shrubs have greedy roots (birch and privet are particularly bad) and bulbs planted beneath them should be given additional fertilizer, such as bonemeal or Growmore, forked into the surface in early spring.

In containers

Many dwarf bulbs thrive in troughs and sinks, together with alpines, and share their liking for sharply drained soil and an open sunny site. Their dainty attractions can also be appreciated in such a setting. The smallest and least invasive bulbs should be chosen, so that they do not dominate or overwhelm their neighbours, and those with unobtrusive foliage which does not look too untidy after flowering are preferable. The dwarfest crocuses, cyclamen and rhodohypoxis would be good candidates.

Many of the easily grown dwarf bulbs can be used to provide early colour in ornamental containers, such as pots and urns on a patio and window boxes. The commoner crocuses, daffodils, grape hyacinths, scillas, Reticulata irises and tulips are all suitable. If they are to be followed by other plants, they should be lifted when the leaves begin to die down and then either planted out in the garden, or kept in a cool dry place for replanting in the autumn in the containers.

Under glass

Although most of the bulbs described in this book will succeed in the open garden and few require protection from cold, some can be grown to advantage under glass, either in an unheated greenhouse or in a frame. This shelters them from excessive rain in winter, keeps the blooms in pristine condition, which is especially valuable with very early-flowering or tiny plants, and provides the relatively dry dormant period after flowering to which so many bulbs are accustomed in their natural habitats. Among those recommended for cultivation under glass are small-flowered colchicums, Juno irises, the slightly tender cyclamen, Jonquil narcissus, less common species of crocus, leucojum, tulip and fritillary and such little-known genera as *Calochortus* and *Habranthus*.

There are two methods of growing bulbs under glass – either in pots or planted in a bed – and in both cases they can be covered with a frame or Dutch lights or kept in a cold greenhouse. A suitable compost for the pots is John Innes No. 2, with a third of its bulk of grit added; alternatively, a home-made compost can be prepared, consisting of two parts loam, preferably sterilized, one part peat and one and a half parts grit, plus 8 oz (225 g) John Innes base fertilizer and 4 oz (110 g) lime to the bushel (8 gallons; 36 litres). A well-drained peat-based compost, with extra grit incorporated, is another possibility. Clay or plastic pots may be used: the former minimize the risk of overwatering, but are best plunged in sand to prevent them drying out too quickly.

Above: 'Cream Beauty' (left), one of the several robust hybrids of *Crocus chrysanthus*; *Calochortus venustus* (right) a choice summer-flowering bulb for a warm spot

Below: *Cyclamen coum* and winter aconites, *Eranthis hyemalis*, enjoy the dappled shade of shrubs and trees and both self-sow freely

The bulbs should be potted as soon as they can be obtained in late summer, ideally in September or early October, and planted at about three times their own depth or, for large bulbs, about a third of the way up the pot. After planting, they should be top dressed with grit and kept watered until growth dies down in May. Many of the trickier bulbs, such as some fritillaries and tulips, benefit from a summer drying off period, without any water at all. They can then be repotted if they are becoming over-crowded, or top dressed with fresh potting compost, before being started into growth again in September.

For planting bulbs in a bed with overhead protection, be it in a frame or cold greenhouse, a similar compost is suitable, again ensuring that it is well-drained. In a frame, the bed should be raised above ground level to improve drainage. This will create a "bulb frame", which is simply a raised bed covered with frame lights. Many bulbs increase and grow more vigorously if planted in a bed, the main disadvantage being the difficulty of retrieving them if they need to be lifted when dormant. To overcome this, growers often put the choicer bulbs in plastic lattice pots (of the type used for aquatic plants) plunged in the bed; another solution is to separate the different groups with vertical tiles or slates. After the first year, bonemeal should be forked into the surface every spring.

PROPAGATION

Most of the common bulbs increase freely of their own accord, by splitting into two or more bulbs, like many daffodils, or by forming small bulbils around the base of the parent bulb, a feature of many Reticulata irises and fritillaries. These may be carefully separated or detached and planted individually. On the other hand, many of the less common bulbs do not increase readily in this way, but do set seed.

Although gardeners seem reluctant to grow bulbs from seed, the technique is not difficult and requires only a modicum of patience. The majority of bulbs will flower within three years of sowing and few take longer than five years – time which passes quickly if more species are sown each year, so that there are always new arrivals to be enjoyed.

Seed usually ripens by midsummer and should be sown as early as possible in the autumn, in John Innes seed compost or a peat-based compost with good drainage. Sow the seeds fairly thinly, just cover them with compost and finish with a layer of chippings at least ¼ in. (0.5 cm) thick. Put the pots outside in a shady place and keep moist until the seeds germinate, after which they can be

Like many Reticulata irises, *I. histriodes* 'Major' increases freely from offsets

---

brought into a frame or cold greenhouse or at least be exposed to more light. The seedlings can normally be kept in the original pots for two growing seasons, allowing them to dry off when the foliage dies down and starting to water again in September. Some seed, especially if it is not sown until after Christmas, may not germinate for a further year and in this case the compost should be kept moist throughout. After two years, the young bulbs can be either repotted in the same way as adult bulbs or, if they are reasonably large, planted in the garden.

PESTS AND DISEASES

Pest and diseases generally cause few problems with bulbous plants, especially when they are grown in the open garden, but some of the more common are listed here.

Slugs can damage young growth, especially in damp conditions, and underground they may damage the bulbs themselves. Any of the slug killers available, as pellets or liquid preparations, can be used effectively.

Aphids are rarely troublesome except under glass. They should be treated as soon as they are seen with dimethoate, heptenophos or pirimicarb, since they can weaken the plants and are responsible for the spread of viruses (see below). Red spider mite only affects bulbs grown under glass, particularly if the atmosphere has been allowed to become very dry. If a severe infestation occurs, frequent spraying with pirimiphos-methyl, malathion or dimethoate will be necessary. Pesticide resistance is nowadays widespread so a better alternative is to introduce the predatory mite, *Phytoseiulus persimilis* in the late spring when spider mite becomes active. It is available from Defenders Ltd, PO Box 131, Wye, Kent TN25 5TQ; English Woodlands Biocontrol, Hoyle Depot, Graffham, Petworth, W. Sussex, GU28 0LR; Natural Pest Control, Yapton Road, Barnham, Bognor Regis, W. Sussex, PO22 0BQ; Wyebugs, Department of Biological Sciences, Wye College, Ashford, Kent, TN25 5AH.

Vine weevil can be a serious pest with pot-grown bulbs, especially cyclamen and begonia. Sterilized compost should be used and, if the grubs, which have curved plump white bodies and brown heads, are seen, the compost should be removed from around the bulbs and the grubs killed. Fresh compost should then be used incorporating gamma-HCH dust. Plants can also be protected by drenching the compost with a pathogenic nematode (*Heterorhabditis* sp.) in late summer. This is available from the above addresses and is likely to be more effective than the insecticides available to amateur gardeners.

Lily beetle is becoming increasingly common in certain parts of the country, notable Surrey and the surrounding counties, and can cause severe damage to the leaves of fritillaries, as well as lilies. The beetles, which are bright red and about $\frac{1}{3}$ in. (8mm) long, and their reddish grubs covered in black excrement should be picked off whenever they are seen. Regular spraying with permethrin, pirimiphos-methyl or fenitrothion is also effective.

Two other pests, the large narcissus bulb fly and stem and bulb eelworm, are difficult to control. Destroy affected plants. Birds and mice can be destructive in some gardens, see p. 148.

Botrytis occasionally affects bulbs, especially under glass, fritillaries, tulips and irises being the most frequently attacked. The earliest sign is usually the development of grey spots on the leaves, which spread rapidly to the whole plant. Spraying with benomyl or carbendazim is normally effective but too regular use could lead to the build up of resistance.

Virus disease is more likely to worry the specialist grower than the average gardener. Micropropagation has made it possible to achieve virus-free stocks and plants grown from seed are also virus-free, which may eventually ensure that all stocks are healthy. In the meantime, affected plants should be destroyed and regular spraying against aphids should prevent spread of the disease.

Crocus

Crocuses are among the most widely grown dwarf bulbs for the spring garden, but their popularity rests mainly on the large-flowered Dutch hybrids, listed in a wide range of varieties in every bulb catalogue. These are easily grown in sun or partial shade in most soils and will even thrive in grass, as long as the leaves are allowed to die down before cutting it. Most catalogues give adequate descriptions of the colours and variations in flowering period and individual descriptions would be superfluous here.

The genus is a large one and the numerous species now in cultivation have a delicate charm lacking in the familiar Dutch hybrids. Many are easily grown and sufficiently prodigal in their increase to provide good patches of colour in the garden, while those requiring a little extra care can easily be grown in a frame or unheated greenhouse. Few genera can provide colour for such a long period, from August until May.

The majority of crocuses grow well in an open sunny situation in well-drained soil. A rock garden is ideal, but any position where they can be appreciated in spite of their small size is suitable, especially if the drainage has been improved by incorporating extra grit.

Many crocuses increase well by division and some will self-sow themselves around after a year or two. However, it is always worthwhile looking for seed of the less common species, which can be expected to flower in three or four years from sowing. The ripe seed capsules are frequently hidden at ground level and need searching for among the dying leaves.

Diseases are rarely a problem, but pests can be troublesome. Whether in the garden or under glass, the corms seem to be particularly appetizing to mice and in some woodland gardens are equally popular with squirrels. An enthusiastic mouse-catching cat can work wonders, otherwise traps may be effective. In a frame, mice can be kept at bay by lining it with fine mesh netting. Birds are another nuisance and often treat crocuses, especially yellow varieties, in the same way as primroses and polyanthus, nipping through the flower stems at or above ground level. Apart from avoiding crocuses which are likely targets, the only answer is bird netting or, less conspicuously, black cotton.

The following list contains a selection of species and cultivars which are obtainable from the trade and which should succeed in the open garden. For the ever-increasing number of crocus enthusiasts, there is further information about the rarer species in specialist books.

AUTUMN-FLOWERING

Many of the autumn-flowering crocuses resemble the colchicums, in that they produce their flowers before the leaves appear, in October and November, generally in shades of pale to deep lavender or white and often with conspicuous orange anthers. This description fits the two vigorous large-flowered species most commonly seen in the catalogues – Crocus speciosus, and C. kotschyanus (frequently listed as C. zonatus). The latter has pale lilac flowers with two yellow spots at the base of each segment, while its variety leucopharynx (C. karduchorum) has a pure white throat and tube and is one of the most beautiful of all crocuses, increasing well in the garden. C. speciosus is more variable and several cultivars have been named, including the white 'Albus', deep violet 'Oxonian' and the very large, pale 'Aitchisonii'.

Also similar in their colour range and absence of leaves at flowering time are Crocus medius, C. nudiflorus and C. pulchellus. C. nudiflorus has darker flowers than the others and is unusual in being stoloniferous, so that it usually builds up a colony quite quickly. 'Zephyr', a cultivar of C. pulchellus, is very vigorous and has exceptionally pale flowers.

One species deserving special mention is Crocus banaticus, known as C. iridiflorus in the past because of the intriguing iris-like flowers, in which the inner segments are small and tend to curve in, whereas the outer segments spread outwards or recurve. The beauty of the pale lavender flowers is enhanced by the conspicuous, branching, white anthers. Although still expensive, this is an easy plant in a situation which does not get too dry and it increases freely.

Several autumn-flowering crocuses develop their leaves to a greater or lesser degree by the time the flowers appear, giving an appearance quite different from the naked flowers of those already described. The colour range is again similar. The saffron crocus, Crocus sativus, is typical, having abundant leaves and lilac flowers heavily veined with purple, with striking red anthers. Unfortunately, the flowers are not readily produced in Britain and the smaller-flowered C. cartwrightianus and robust C. serotinus subsp. salzmannii are more floriferous plants. Into this group, of which the nomenclature is confusing, probably falls the crocus called in catalogues *C. asturicus* 'Atropurpureus', with an excellent deep purple flower.

Another species occasionally offered is *Crocus laevigatus*, which varies considerably from white to lavender but usually has beautiful dark veining. Its much more vigorous cultivar, 'Fontenayi', is easily grown and flowers into December. The finest of these crocuses is *C. goulimyi*, which was discovered in southern Greece as recently as 1955 and is rapidly becoming a garden favourite. It has a somewhat globular, pale lavender flower with a white throat and an exceptionally long tube. There is also a lovely pure white variety and both will increase happily in the garden. There are several other white autumn-flowering species. The two easiest and most readily available are *Crocus ochroleucus* and *C. hadriaticus*, the former having a yellow throat.

WINTER- AND SPRING-FLOWERING

The crocuses already described flower mainly in October and November and may produce occasional flowers in December, to coincide with the earliest of the winter- and spring-flowering species. There are three that can be relied upon to start flowering in January in normal weather conditions. *Crocus imperati* is usually the first – a beautiful plant whose large flowers are deep purple when they open in the sunshine, but buff-coloured with dark feathering on the outside of the unopened buds. A striking contrast is provided by *C. fleischeri*, which has small, pure white flowers with prominent, large, red anthers. Although delicate in appearance, it withstands the weather well and is a good garden plant. The earliest of the yellow crocuses generally starts flowering in January. This is *C. ancyrensis*, with small flowers sometimes marked brown on the outside of the petals.

Depending on the weather, the main flowering period of crocuses is February to March, with a few late species carrying on the display in April. Following *Crocus ancyrensis*, there are a number of others with deep yellow flowers, some with conspicuous brown or purple markings. The popular *C. flavus* (*C. aureus*) is very vigorous and freely increasing, especially in the clone generally

Opposite, top: *Crocus speciosus* (left) and *C. kotschyanus* (right) are the best-known autumn-flowering species

Centre: *C. fleischeri* (left) and *C. ancyrensis* (right) are especially valuable for their winter blooms

Bottom: *C.* 'Hubert Edelsten' (left) and *C. alexandri* (right) are both distinctive for their colouring

available in the trade, which has larger flowers than the wild species. Unfortunately, this is the crocus most likely to have its flowers demolished by birds.

A clear yellow species with large flowers, *Crocus chrysanthus* is best known as the parent of many excellent robust hybrids, such as 'Blue Pearl' and 'Blue Bird' among the blues, 'Cream Beauty', a soft, creamy yellow, 'E. A. Bowles' and 'Gypsy Girl' in deeper yellow and the white 'Snow Bunting' and 'Ladykiller', the latter having deep purple on the outside of the petals. *C. olivieri* has deep yellow or orange flowers, normally unmarked, although the more frequently offered subspecies *balansae*, which is almost identical, is heavily streaked with brown.

There are several spring-flowering species in shades of lavender or purple, often with attractive darker feathering. The commonest by far is *Crocus tommasinianus*, which has lavender-blue flowers with white throats and increases so prodigiously by division and by seed that its planting may be regretted, except perhaps in grass. However, these strictures do not apply to the white form, 'Albus', or the dark purple 'Whitwell Purple', which are both well worth growing.

The popular *Crocus dalmaticus* is pale purple with a brownish tinge on the outside. The variable *C. vernus* generally has flowers in shades of lavender, while the equally variable *C. sieberi* tends to have a deep orange throat. In the variety *tricolor*, this is separated form the pale purple tips by a white band – a dramatic colour combination – and the hybrid 'Hubert Edelsten' also has an unusual mixture of white and reddish purple.

Two species with pale purple flowers notable for their dark feathering, particularly in bud, are the very similar *Crocus minimus* and *C. corsicus*. The most obvious difference to the gardener is that *C. minimus* is one of the earliest and *C. corsicus* one of the latest to flower. Of the botanically complicated *C. biflorus*, nurserymen generally offer *C. biflorus* subsp. *biflorus*, which is white with extensive purple streaking on the outside of the segments, and two other subspecies – the striking *alexandri*, with a dark violet band on the reverse, and *weldenii*, in which the outside of the segments is suffused with brownish grey.

Colchicum

Although commonly called autumn crocus, this genus differs from crocus both botanically and horticulturally. Whereas crocuses belong to the iris family and have three stamens and a symmetrical corm, colchicums belong to the lily family and have six stamens and an irregular elongated corm with a flattened projection below the point of exit of the roots, which is at the side of the corm. From the gardener's point of view, the most important distinction is that the leaves of most autumn-flowering colchicums are very large and, appearing in the spring after the flowers, persist late into the summer. The colour too is often a shade of pink, deeper or paler, which is not often seen in crocuses. Colchicums may be propagated by division of the corms or from seed.

Most of the commonly available large-leaved colchicums flower from August to October or November and are easy to grow in sun or semi-shade, but their placing in the garden is less easy than with crocuses whose leaves are insignificant and disappear quickly. A compromise is needed between a position where the comparatively small crocus-like flowers can be appreciated and one where the persistent cabbage-like leaves cannot damage other low plants. The most vigorous colchicums will grow in rough grass, but mowing or scything then has to be left very late, until the foliage has died down. The ideal situation is probably towards the front of a shrub border, where no other ground-covering plants are used. In addition to the well-known colchicums of this kind, there are several small-leaved delicate species, mostly spring-flowering, for which cultivation under glass is advisable.

The two commonest species offered in catalogues are *Colchicum autumnale* and *C. speciosum*. The former is the one often known confusingly as autumn crocus or meadow saffron and has lilac-pink flowers, but there are white and double forms, *album* and 'Pleniflorum', as well as the closely related, deep purple *C. atropurpureum*. *C. speciosum* is a magnificent species with much larger, pink flowers and a number of named forms, of which 'Album' is an exceptionally fine (and expensive) white. *C. cilicium* resembles a larger-flowered *C. autumnale* with very big leaves and *C. macrophyllum* is similar with perhaps the largest leaves of all, up to 20 in. (50 cm) long and 6 in. (15 cm) wide. Some species have a darker chequering on the segments, which adds to their

Colchicum speciosum (left) and its exquisite white-flowered form,
'Album' (right); the flowers are showy enough to compensate for the
large leaves which follow

attractiveness. This is well marked in *Colchicum agrippinum*,
C. bivonae (*C. bowlesianum*) and *C. sibthorpii*.

A number of colchicums have smaller flowers and relatively insignificant leaves, but they are less easy to grow and more liable
to be damaged by the weather. However, they make excellent pot
or frame plants. They include two similar autumn-flowering
species – *Colchicum boissieri* and *C. cupanii*, which both have
small, unchequered, pink flowers with a white tube and throat,
the latter being unusual in producing leaves at the same time. The
small spring-flowering species are generally too frail to be grown
outside and only available from specialist nurseries. Among them
are the rare *Colchicum luteum*, unique in the genus in having deep
yellow flowers, and *C. hungaricum*, one of the most reliable dwarf
species, bearing palest pink or white flowers with conspicuous
chocolate-coloured anthers from January to March.

Galanthus

Most gardeners grow and love snowdrops, whether in occasional groups tucked beneath shrubs and soon forgotten after flowering, or naturalized by the thousand in woodland. The true galanthophile recognizes some 20 species of *Galanthus* and perhaps over 100 varieties, often varying only slightly in size, shape and in the number of green markings on the segments. Generally speaking, they are 3 to 5 in. (8–12 cm) high. A few of the more distinct kinds are described here and the enthusiast should refer to the specialist literature and catalogues.

Snowdrops generally grow best in partial or full shade under trees or shrubs, as long as the soil is not too dry, although a few prefer a sunnier position in well-drained soil. Unlike so many shade-lovers, they thrive on alkaline soils. They differ from the majority of bulbs in establishing most successfully when they are planted in growth or "in the green", preferably after flowering; for this reason, the cheap dry bulbs available for planting in autumn may not prove a good investment. Snowdrops are easily propagated from seed or by dividing clumps of bulbs.

The season starts, surprisingly, in the autumn, with *Galanthus nivalis* subsp. *reginae-olgae* (sometimes offered as *G. corcyrensis* or *G. reginae-olgae*). The flowers appear before the leaves in the earliest forms and it grows well in the open garden, especially if given a sunny spot with well-drained soil.

Galanthus nivalis 'Lutescens' (left), an unusual but frailer form of the common snowdrop; the large-flowered *G. elwesii* (right) is sometimes slower to establish than *G. nivalis*

Galanthus caucasicus has noticeably grey leaves and large blooms

The common snowdrop, *Galanthus nivalis*, itself is the most widely used species for naturalizing and has a large number of forms, of which the double, with its muddled, green-flecked centre, is almost equally easily grown. 'Viridapicis' has much more green than normal on the inner segments. 'Lutescens' and 'Flavescens' are very distinct in having yellow markings instead of green, but they are less robust and do not increase so freely. 'Magnet' is unusual in carrying its flowers on very long, curving pedicels. 'Atkinsii' is a vigorous hybrid between *G. nivalis* and *G. plicatus*, some 6 in. (15 cm) or more tall.

There are several larger snowdrops, of which *Galanthus elwesii* is the commonest and one of the best garden plants. It has very broad, glaucous-grey leaves and large flowers, frequently appearing earlier than those of *G. nivalis*, but does not increase quite so readily. Other large-flowered species which are usually available are *G. byzantinus*, *G. caucasicus* and *G. plicatus*, differing a little in the greyness of the leaves, in the folding of the leaf edges and in the green markings on the segments.

All the snowdrops mentioned so far have grey-green leaves, but there are at least two which are distinct in having glossy green leaves. The most often seen are *G. ikariae* and its subspecies *latifolius*, which are easy to grow and increase well in a sunny well-drained position.

Leucojum

Leucojum is a neglected genus compared with *Galanthus*, but several snowflakes are trouble-free garden plants which deserve to be better known, while the remainder are excellent for growing under glass.

The best species for the garden are *Leucojum vernum*, flowering in the spring, *L. aestivum* in early summer and *L. autumnale* in autumn. These all do well in partial shade or in sun and present no difficulties, the first two even growing satisfactorily in grass. The spring snowflake, *L. vernum*, has glossy green leaves and stems 3 to 6 in. (8–15 cm) high, carrying one or two exquisite, cup-shaped, nodding flowers, pure white with green tips to the segments. The variety *carpathicum* differs only in having yellow tips instead of green. Flowering usually starts at the end of January or early February, whereas the summer snowflake, *L. aestivum*, flowers in late April or early May. It is a much taller plant, with stems up to 12 in. (30 cm), or even more in the clone 'Gravetye Giant'. The leaves too are longer and narrower and the flowers smaller, but with up to six on a stem.

The autumn-flowering *Leucojum autumnale* is very different, with long slender leaves and 4 in. (10 cm) reddish stems, each bearing one or two small, white, bell-shaped flowers in September

Leucojum vernum is an undemanding plant which flourishes in many different situations

The summer snowflake, *Leucojum aestivum*, does particularly well near water

and October. Its delicate appearance belies its vigour and it will soon build up into a good clump in partial shade or full sun. The rare *L. roseum* is like a miniature edition of *L. autumnale*, with pink-flushed flowers also produced in autumn. It merits cultivation under glass, as do the little spring-flowering species, *L. nicaeense*, *L. longifolium* and *L. trichophyllum*, all requiring full sun and having small white bells on 2 to 4 in. (5–10 cm) stems. Of these, *L. nicaeense* is certainly the easiest, a splendid, freely increasing pot plant.

Iris

Among the dwarf irises are some of the most exquisite spring-flowering bulbs. They fall mainly into two botanical sections of the genus, Juno and Reticulata.

RETICULATA IRISES

The Reticulata section contains many easy and beautiful plants less than 6 in. (15 cm) high, demanding only a sunny position and reasonable drainage and flowering from January to March. They usually increase by offsets, which can be detached and planted separately or left to develop into clumps. They have few troubles apart from ink spot disease, a serious fungal infection which can take hold in gardens where large numbers of Reticulata irises are grown. Affected bulbs have dark inky patches on them and should be destroyed; the leaves of surviving plants should be sprayed with mancozeb during the growing season. Ink spot disease is not common and should not deter gardeners from trying Reticulata irises.

The most widely-grown of this section is *Iris reticulata* itself, together with its various hybrids and cultivars found in bulb catalogues. The species has deep violet-blue flowers with a yellow central crest and white streaks at the base of the falls (the outer segments of the iris flower). In the variety *krelagei* the colour is a uniform reddish purple and the robust 'J. S. Dijt' is similar. 'Cantab' has a base colour of pale blue, again with a yellow crest surrounded with white. 'Clairette' is a striking form, pale blue but with a deep violet blade (the lowest portion of the fall) and a white crest with dark streaks each side of it. There are several others with deep blue flowers, which may well be hybrids with *I. histrioides*; they are exceptionally vigorous plants and increase very freely in the garden, the two best known being 'Harmony' and 'Joyce'.

The beautiful *Iris bakeriana* has pale blue flowers with a dark blue blade and conspicuous yellow crest. In the garden it enjoys the same conditions as other Reticulatas, but is less robust.

The most cheerful sight of the winter garden is the splash of colour from *Iris histrioides* 'Major', which generally opens its large, remarkably weather-resistant flowers in January. They are

'Cantab' (above) and 'Harmony' (below), two lovely and dependable Reticulata irises

very deep blue with a yellow crest with white streaks on each side of it and they last for several weeks. A much more difficult plant, probably only suitable for cultivation under glass, is *I. histrio*, but its variety *aintabensis* is widely available and a good garden plant, with smaller, pale blue flowers. There are two yellow-flowered Reticulata irises. Grown in vast quantity by Dutch nurserymen, *Iris danfordiae* is not a very satisfactory garden plant because, after flowering well in the first season, it then splits into small bulbils and does not flower again. Planting the bulbs at least 10 in. (25 cm) deep may discourage splitting and help to overcome this. The flower shape is unusual, with tiny standards (inner segments) and falls sloping upwards, giving a squat bunched appearance. *I. winogradowii* has only recently become obtainable in the trade and is a magnificent plant, with large yellow flowers of similar size and shape to *I. histrioides* 'Major', generally not produced until March. Although growing reasonably in sun, it seems to do better in a partially shaded position with additional humus in the soil.

Hybrids have been raised between *Iris histrioides* and *I. winogradowii*. The commonest of these is an extremely vigorous plant, 'Katharine Hodgkin', which has very large flowers of a curious greenish yellow, heavily streaked and spotted with blue. These usually appear in February, when the flowers of *I. histrioides* are going over.

JUNO IRISES

The Juno irises, flowering between February and April, are less widely grown because of their special requirements. Most of the smaller species are tricky and only suitable for cultivation under glass, since they need a dry period during the summer months and resent excessive moisture on their leaves at other times. This applies to the delightful yellow-flowered *I. caucasica*, which is one of the easier dwarf species, and the rarer and more difficult *I. persica*, in various greyish or yellowish shades, with deep purple or brown on the falls, and *I. nusairiensis*, with pale blue flowers.

Among the larger Juno irises are several strong-growing species which can be grown in the open garden, given a well-drained hot position, perhaps at the foot of a south-facing wall which shields them from rain in summer. One of the easiest is *Iris bucharica*, generally 1 ft (30 cm) high with lush leaves, from the axils of which arises a succession of flowers, white with yellow falls. *I. magnifica*, with white or pale blue flowers, is similar, but

Iris winogradowii (left), a rare species until recently but now proving very hardy; its hybrid, *I.* 'Katharine Hodgkin' (right), is also becoming more widely available

---

may attain up to 2 ft (60 cm) in height. Other tall species include *I. aucheri* (*I. sindjarensis*) and *I. graeberiana*, with deep blue flowers.

All these can be grown outside, at least in the south, but it is always most important to start with sound bulbs. The bulb itself is unusual in having a number of permanent thickened storage roots beneath it, which seem to be essential for it to become established and which are frequently broken off through careless handling. Propagation of Juno irises is usually by seed, although some vigorous species will increase by division.

Opposite: the aptly named *Iris magnifica* in front of a south-facing wall

Daffodils are among the most popular of all garden plants, although the species themselves and the smaller hybrids seem to be less appreciated than the vast array of large-flowered cultivars. Most of them are just as easily grown and have the same gift of remaining in pristine condition for several weeks during cool weather. As the foliage is less obtrusive than in their larger relations, they are more suitable for planting at the front of a border or in the rock garden and many will do well in partial shade, irrespective of how acid or alkaline the soil is. A few will grow in grass, but on the whole the larger daffodils are better for this purpose. Daffodils vary in their cultural requirements, which will be discussed below, but unless otherwise stated, it can be assumed that they will grow in any reasonable soil in an open position. (See also the Wisley Handbook, *Daffodils*.)

There are several miniatures of the typical trumpet daffodil, both species and hybrids. The smallest is *Narcissus asturiensis* (*N. minimus*), usually only 2 to 3 in. (5–8 cm) high with deep yellow flowers in proportion. Like all this group, it is easy to grow in the open garden and will tolerate a certain amount of shade. The similar but larger and later-flowering *N. minor* has stems

The diminutive *Narcissus asturienis* comes from northern Spain, where it may be found growing in snow

Narcissus 'Hawera', a delightful Triandus hybrid from New Zealand

generally around 6 in. (15 cm). *N. pseudonarcissus* is the wild daffodil widely distributed throughout Europe including Britain, where it is known as the Lent lily or Tenby daffodil. It has a number of named subspecies and varieties, ranging in height from 6 to 12 in. (15–30 cm) and varying in depth of colour and in the carriage of the trumpet-shaped flower, which may be horizontal or more pendulous. Two very distinct subspecies are *pallidiflorus* and *moschatus*. The first grows to about 8 in. (20 cm), with large flowers of a delicate creamy yellow. It seems to thrive in semi-shade with plenty of humus in the soil and increases slowly. The second has off-white hanging flowers and likes the same conditions.

Among the small trumpet hybrids are 'Bambi', only 6 in. (15 cm) high with creamy white petals and deep yellow trumpets, and 'W. P. Milner', which has creamy flowers on 10 in. (25 cm) stems. Other similar cultivars can be found in specialist catalogues.

The aptly named angel's tears, *Narcissus triandrus*, is an exquisite species whose pendulous flowers have long cups and recurving petals – a beautiful shape which it has imparted to its hybrids. It usually appears in catalogues as *N. triandrus* 'Albus', with creamy white flowers, and there is also a subspecies *pallidulus* (generally offered as *N. concolor*) with deep yellow flowers.

165

Narcissus cyclamineus, a fine species in its own right and also the parent of many outstanding hybrids

Both grow well in sun or light shade, in well-drained soil containing abundant humus.

Many of the Triandrus hybrids are a little tall to be included here, but two dwarfs with several graceful, nodding flowers to a stem are the golden 'April Tears' and pale lemon 'Hawera'.

Narcissus cyclamineus is a fine species requiring moist, preferably semi-shaded conditions, in which it may well become naturalized, increasing by division and by seed. The flower is elongated, with a long narrow trumpet and distinctive, swept back petals of similar length. It has proved a prolific parent of hybrids of all sizes, mostly with petals reflexed to some degree. The best known is probably 'Tête-à-Tête', 6 to 8 in. (15–20 cm) high with beautiful, long-lasting, deep yellow flowers, generally produced in early March and increasing very freely indeed. 'Jack Snipe' is a little taller, with a yellow cup and cream reflexed petals, and 'Beryl' has an orange cup and primrose petals. Of the larger Cyclamineus hybrids about 12 in. (30 cm) high, 'February Gold', 'February Silver', 'March Sunshine' and 'Jenny' are outstanding easy plants, the first three normally flowering in March (in spite of their names) and 'Jenny' in April.

Many species in the Jonquil group need a warm sunny position in well-drained soil; alternatively, they make excellent pot plants

The hoop-petticoat daffodil, *Narcissus bulbocodium*, seeds itself freely and will form colonies even in grass

for an unheated greenhouse or frame, benefiting from a dry period in the summer. All have fragrant flowers with small cups and petals held at right angles to them, but they differ considerably in height and in the number of flowers to a stem. *Narcissus rupicola* usually bears solitary flowers of deep yellow, as does its uncommon subspecies *marvieri*, with larger flowers. The smallest species, *N. scaberulus* and *N. gaditanus*, are only about 2 to 3 in. (5–8 cm), with several flowers on a stem. *N. assoanus* (*N. requienii*, *N. juncifolius*) is taller, up to 6 in. (15 cm), as is the more robust *N. jonquilla* itself and the slightly smaller variety *henriquesii*. A number of others are of similar height to this, 6 to 8 in. (15–20 cm), including *N. fernandesii* and *N. willkommii*.

Most members of the Tazetta group – the popular "narcissi" with clusters of scented flowers – are too large to be considered here, apart from *Narcissus canaliculatus* (*N. tazetta* subsp. *italicus*), a delightful 5 in. (12 cm) dwarf, with white petals and a yellow cup. It does best in a hot sunny spot. The hybrid, 'Minnow', is only a little taller, having cream-coloured flowers with yellow cups, and is less demanding of warmth than the species itself.

The hoop-petticoat daffodils, *Narcissus bulbocodium* and its allies, are some of the loveliest dwarf narcissus. Although varying greatly in height and colour, all have the characteristic, large,

Narcissus cantabricus var. *petunioides* is unfortunately rather scarce in cultivation

funnel-shaped cup framed with very small, unobtrusive petals. *N. bulbocodium* itself and its varieties *obesus* and *conspicuus* are among the most vigorous and grow well in the open garden or even in grass, as at the RHS Garden at Wisley where they are a wonderful sight in early spring. These usually have deep yellow flowers, while the equally vigorous var. *citrinus* is pale primrose. The smallest variety is the very early-flowering *nivalis*, some 3 in. (8 cm) high, which is probably best with glass protection. *N. romieuxii* also flowers extremely early, in January or even before, and is often recommended for cultivation under glass, but does well in the open in a sunny well-drained position and increases readily. The flowers are pale yellow with protuberant stamens.

The species *Narcissus cantabricus* and its relatives are very similar to *N. bulbocodium*, with white flowers, and originate from southern Spain and North Africa. They are dwarf, early and very beautiful, but do best under glass with a summer drying-off period. The finest of all is *N. cantabricus* var. *petunioides*, in which the cup is flared out to the horizontal – a most unusual shape. 'Julia Jane' resembles it, but in pale yellow.

Tulipa

The large hybrid tulips, which have been developed so magnificently over the centuries by Dutch growers, now bear little resemblance to the wild species and it is among the latter that almost all the dwarf tulips are found. To many gardeners, tulips seem too formal for anything but bedding and they rarely make good garden plants if left alone in a permanent position like daffodils. However, whereas the dwarf narcissus species are usually a little more difficult to grow than the hybrids, the reverse seems to be the case with tulips and there are many delightful species under 12 in. (30 cm) in height which persist and increase when planted in the open garden.

With only one exception, tulips need an open sunny site and a well-drained soil. The rock garden or a raised bed are therefore ideal positions for the smaller ones and the front of a sunny border for the larger. Some species are reluctant to increase by division and can only be propagated by seed, which takes from four to six years to attain flowering size.

The tulips described here are generally available from nurserymen and make satisfactory garden plants, at least in the south of England. Some of the rarer species occasionally offered do better under glass, where they can be given the summer drying-off period which they receive in nature, and this treatment will suit any of the species in colder areas. They offer a wide range of colours, from white and yellow through pink to purple and shades of scarlet, frequently with a contrasting colour on the outside of the petals. The main flowering time is April.

Tulipa biflora is a small species roughly 4 in. (10 cm) high, with up to three flowers to a stem, white with yellow at the base and tinged grey on the outside. Of somewhat similar colouring are *T. polychroma* and *T. turkestanica*, the latter with conspicuous brown anthers.

The lady tulip, *Tulipa clusiana*, is one of the most beautiful of all, about 6 to 8 in. (15–20 cm) high, with a starry white flower stained deep rose on the outside. The variety *chrysantha* (*T. chrysantha*) differs only in having a yellow base colour. Another easily grown species of similar size is *T. tarda* (*T. dasystemon*); the white flowers in April and May have at least the inner third of each petal yellow and greenish shading on the reverse.

The only tulip flourishing in shady conditions is *Tulipa*

169

sylvestris, naturalized in parts of England. It is an easy garden plant which increases freely when planted among shrubs, although it is sometimes shy to flower. The flowers are yellow with green outside and tend, in shade, to have outward-curving stems.

A first-class rock garden plant some 4 to 6 in. (10–15 cm) high, *Tulipa urumiensis* has large, short-stemmed, yellow flowers streaked externally with bronze. *T. batalinii* is another very good large-flowered dwarf, the colour a soft creamy yellow. It is probably a subspecies of the red *T. linifolia* (p. 172).

Pinks and purples are represented in the highly variable species, *Tulipa humilis*, under which are included *T. pulchella*, *T. violacea* and *T. aucheriana*. The colour of *T. humilis* in the wild ranges from light pink to deep purple, usually with a central yellow blotch. In cultivation, the paler colours are generally seen in *T. humilis* and *T. pulchella*, the darker in *T. violacea*. A delightful, easily grown dwarf *T. aucheriana*, is only 3 to 4 in. (8–10 cm) high, with pink flowers with a yellow centre. The rare *T. violacea* var. *pallida* is particularly striking, white with a deep violet blotch. All are very early flowering, in February and March, but can be grown in the open.

Tulipa saxatilis and the very similar *T. bakeri* flower later, normally in April, and have glossy green leaves and 8 in. (20 cm) stems bearing one to three large pink flowers. The bulbs are stoloniferous and rapidly form a large colony, which unfortunately does not flower freely until well established. In this respect, *T. bakeri* seems to be a more satisfactory plant than *T. saxatilis*. *T. cretica* is an excellent miniature of these, with a reputation for tenderness which it does not seem to deserve in the south, although it may be safer under glass in the colder counties.

Many of the red-flowered species are slightly large to be considered dwarf bulbs, but nevertheless are good garden plants, for example, *Tulipa eichleri*, *T. fosteriana*, *T. praestans*, *T. greigii* and the magnificent *T. sprengeri*, which is easily grown and one of the latest to flower, often at the end of May. Much smaller at about 12 in. (30 cm) are *T. hageri*, *T. orphanidea* and *T. whittallii*, whose reddish flowers are heavily marked with bronze or green and consequently less vivid than the pure reds. Among dwarf pure red species are *T. maximowiczii* and *T. linifolia*, which are excellent

Opposite, top: *Tulipa biflora* (left) and *T. turkestanica* (right), two vigorous dwarf tulips

Centre: *T. urumiensis* (left) and *T. batalinii* (right) can be recommended for the rock garden

Bottom: *T. bakeri* (left) and *T. sprengeri* (right) flower at the end of the tulip season

The compact *Tulipa kaufmanniana* produces its large flowers early in the year

plants for the rock garden. Attractive hybrids between *T. linifolia* and the yellow *T. batalinii* are available in shades of creamy bronze or apricot, such as 'Bronze Charm'.

Tulipa greigii is the parent of a large number of spectacular hybrids, often with striped leaves, flowering in March. Some of the best small varieties are 'Ali Baba', pale pink with scarlet interior, 'Donna Bella', pale yellow with a dark base and red exterior, 'Dreamboat', salmon, 'Ontario', pink, 'Plaisir', yellow streaked with red, and 'Red Riding Hood', scarlet.

T. fosteriana has also produced several good hybrids, usually flowering in April, though somewhat tall to be mentioned here at up to 18 in. (45 cm). They include 'Madam Lefeber', bright red, 'Candela', yellow, 'Orange Emperor', orange, and 'Purissima', white.

The hybrids of the waterlily tulip, *T. kaufmanniana*, are splendid garden plants, with flowers which open wide in the sun, on stems of only 6 to 8 in. (15–20 cm), often produced as early as February. In a reasonably well-drained soil, they will persist and even increase better than most other hybrid tulips. The species itself has pale yellow flowers streaked outside with red and is one of the most reliable. Some of the best of the large range of hybrids are 'Alfred Cortot', red, 'Cesar Frank' and 'Gluck', red with yellow inside, 'Chopin' and 'Berlioz', yellow, 'Johann Strauss' and 'The First', white with some red on the reverse, and 'Fritz Kreisler' and 'Heart's Delight', in mixed shades of pink, yellow and red.

Dwarf Bulbs for
Autumn and Winter

Some of the autumn-flowering bulbs have already been described in the chapters on crocus, colchicum, galanthus and leucojum. There are in addition several species of cyclamen, sternbergia and zephyranthes which can be relied upon to flower in the garden at this season.

Many of the hardy cyclamen are easy to grow and can become an increasingly attractive feature of the garden as they multiply from self-sown seed. This applies especially to the autumn-flowering *Cyclamen hederifolium* (*C. neapolitanum*) and the later *C. coum*, which should be planted with their corms just below the surface of the soil in the shade of trees or shrubs and are quite trouble-free. It is always advisable to start with actively growing corms in pots or packed in peat, rather than the cheaper dried corms which may never establish. The soil should be well drained with extra humus incorporated in the form of peat or, better still, leaf mould, which is relished by all cyclamen.

The popular *Cyclamen hederifolium* has pink flowers and attractive dark green leaves with silver patterns; there is also an excellent white variety. Of the other species, *C. cilicium*, with smaller, pale pink flowers, and the related tiny-flowered *C. intaminatum* are hardy in the south at least. So too is *C. mirabile*, which is similar to *C. cilicium*, except that the leaves have a more obvious purple flush and toothed edges. *C. purpurascens* (still better known as *C. europaeum*) has scented pink flowers and is widely available, but seems to lack the vigour of the other hardy species.

The remaining autumn-flowering cyclamen are slightly tender and make fine plants for the cold greenhouse, given a well-drained compost (as described on p. 143), preferably with the addition of sieved leaf mould. *Cyclamen graecum* has beautifully marbled leaves and pale to deep pink flowers, but does not always produce these freely, even with the summer baking which it seems to need more than most species. *C. africanum* resembles a large-leaved *C. hederifolium* and *C. cyprium* has small, white, scented flowers with a pink spot at the base. The uncommon *C. rohlfsianum* bears fragrant, deep crimson flowers in autumn, but is more tender and more difficult to grow.

Sternbergia lutea looks like a deep yellow crocus, about 6 in. (15 cm) high with glossy green leaves appearing with the flowers

Above: The white-flowered variety of the popular and easily grown
Cyclamen hederifolium
Below: *Sternbergia lutea* makes a charming contribution to the autumn
garden

in September and October. It has a reputation for being shy-flowering, although different clones seem to vary in this respect. Plant it in the hottest position possible and leave well alone; the number of flowers should then increase from year to year. The variety *angustifolia* (*S. sicula*) has narrower leaves and is said to be freer-flowering.

Zephyranthes candida is the only hardy member of the genus which is readily available in Britain. It has small crocus-like flowers on 6 in. (15 cm) stems, accompanying long narrow leaves. The flowers are white with a greenish flush at the base.

DECEMBER TO FEBRUARY

Every gardener likes to see a few flowers outside during the winter months and dwarf bulbs can be depended on to produce them, except when there is snow on the ground. Many autumn-flowering bulbs, especially crocuses and cyclamen, will continue to flower sparsely until Christmas and, in a mild season, spring-flowering bulbs such as snowdrops, crocuses and Reticulata irises will be starting before the end of February. There are a number of other dwarf bulbs which will flower in the winter months, particularly January and February, if the weather is not exceptionally harsh.

The winter aconites are well named, their leaves and yellow flowers appearing amazingly quickly with the first spell of good weather in January to make a carpet among shrubs, dividing and self-sowing freely once they are established. *Eranthis hyemalis*, the commonest species, has clear yellow, upturned flowers surrounded with a ruff of narrow leaves. The taller *E*. 'Guinea Gold' has larger flowers and bronzy leaves.

The hardy *Zephyranthes candida* deserves to be more widely grown in British gardens

Above: A carpet of colours provided by the vigorous *Cyclamen coum*
Below: *Anemone blanda* (left) and its forms, such as 'White Splendour'
(right), flower as early as February

The intense blue of *Scilla sibirica* (left) is always welcome in spring;
S. tubergeniana (right) is more restrained, but an enchanting plant

---

Cyclamen coum has the same vigour and favours the same conditions as *C. hederifolium* (p. 173). It generally begins flowering in January and is an immensely variable plant, with numerous related species and subspecies ranging in colour from white to the deepest magenta and having plain or marbled leaves. If several of these are planted together, they will sow themselves around and a galaxy of colours and leaf forms will eventually appear.

The first of the anemones to flower is *Anemone blanda*, a beautiful, easily grown species, especially in partial shade in a limy soil, with deep lavender-blue flowers. There are several excellent named forms offered by nurserymen, among them the much darker 'Atrocaerulea', 'White Splendour' and the pink 'Rosea'. 'Radar' is unusual, being deep magenta-pink with a broad white centre. All these increase gradually from the tubers in rich soil and also seed themselves, flowering after a year or two in a variety of colours, including wishy-washy intermediates unless the named forms are kept well apart.

The earliest of the scillas usually flower in February and make a real impact in the garden with their brilliant blue colour, flourishing and seeding themselves in sun, or in partial shade, where they contrast with snowdrops and aconites. The two best are *Scilla sibirica*, which is usually sold as a selected clone, 'Spring Beauty', with several deep blue flowers on a 3 to 4 in. (8–10 cm) stem, and *S. bifolia* of similar size but with smaller flowers of not quite such a vivid colour. The third common scilla flowering in February is *S. tubergeniana*, which has white flowers with a blue stripe down the centre of each petal.

——— Dwarf Bulbs for Spring ———

As well as the familiar spring-flowering bulbs – narcissus, crocus, iris and tulip – there are many other bulbs belonging to smaller genera which flower at this time, from March to mid-May.

SHADE-LOVERS

Some spring-flowering bulbs, unlike most bulbous plants, need a moist humus-rich soil in semi-shade to thrive. Trillium and erythronium are the most important of these and anemone, fritillaria and cyclamen also contribute several shade-loving species.

Given suitable conditions, the majority of trilliums are easy to grow and once established will form gradually increasing clumps. Those which are widely available are exquisite plants with large three-lobed leaves and three-petalled flowers. The commonest is the wake robin, *Trillium grandiflorum*, which carries sumptuous white flowers well above the leaves in April, growing 8 in. (20 cm) or more in height. A double form, like a formal double camellia in flower shape, can sometimes be obtained and there is also a wonderful pink variety occasionally seen. The slightly smaller *T. ovatum* resembles *T. grandiflorum* and is an equally good, easy garden plant in shade. The flowers are usually smaller and the petals narrower with less overlap.

The interesting *Trillium sessile* has chocolate-brown flowers which are upright and sessile (stalkless) on the broad marbled leaves, while *T. luteum* has greenish yellow flowers. In *T. erectum*,

---

Trillium grandiflorum (left), with glistening white blooms, and its highly desirable pink variety (right)

The curious, upright, dark-coloured flowers of *Trillium erectum*

on the other hand, the flowers are carried on long curved stalks, so that they are horizontal or even nodding. The colour is usually reddish brown and there is also an excellent white variety with a dark centre.

Occasionally offered but unfortunately more difficult to grow, *Trillium undulatum* is similar to *T. erectum* and has generally smaller flowers beautifully striped with dark red. It is about 6 to 9 in. (15–22 cm) high. The much smaller *T. nivale* is only 1 to 2 in. (2–5 cm) high with small white flowers, in some forms heavily speckled with pink. *T. nivale* resembles it, but always has white flowers. Neither are particularly difficult to grow outside and they also make fine pot plants under glass.

Shade-loving plants often seem to have a special delicacy and grace and of no genus is this truer than the erythroniums, curiously named dog's tooth violets: the tubers have some resemblance to dogs' teeth and the flowers remarkably little resemblance to violets! All have exquisite nodding flowers with recurving petals, in a range of colours and with the leaves variously marked or plain. They may be propagated by division or from seed. *Erythronium dens-canis*, from which the common name originates, is certainly the most frequently advertised in nursery catalogues, but is not the best garden plant in most areas, for it often fails to flower well. However, the blotching or mottling of the leaves can be very striking and the flowers are a good pink, with yellow-brown at the base of the petals and dark anthers. It is about 5 in. (12 cm) high. The most satisfactory of the pink-flowered species is the very robust E. revolutum, which has distinctly-marked leaves and pale to deep pink flowers with yellow anthers, increasing well in peaty soil. The less vigorous E. hendersonii has pinkish lavender flowers with a dark centre.

Of the yellow species, Erythronium tuolumnense is one of the best and easiest to grow, with pale green, glossy leaves and one to three deep yellow flowers to a stem. The hybrid, 'Pagoda', is taller, about 8 in. (20 cm) with slightly larger flowers. E. americanum is a very dwarf, yellow species with lovely mottled leaves compensating for its rather shy flowering habit.

Several erythroniums have creamy white flowers, usually with deeper yellow at the base of the petals. Of these, Erythronium oregonum, E. californicum and E. helenae are very similar, up to 8 in. (20 cm) tall, beautiful and easy to grow. The most vigorous of all is 'White Beauty', which may be derived from E. oregonum.

Most anemones thrive in woodland conditions, including the winter-flowering Anemone blanda (p. 177). Our native wood anemone, A. nemorosa, in its better selected forms, is ideal for growing among shrubs and will contend with deep shade. Many named forms can be found in specialist catalogues; some of the best are the double white 'Alboplena', the larger pale blue 'Robinsoniana' and 'Allenii' and the darker 'Royal Blue'. 'Leeds' Variety' is an exceptionally large-flowered, single white and there are one or two named pink forms.

Anemone apennina is very similar to A. blanda with its large, semi-double, pale blue or white flowers, but is more suitable for dense shade, where it will increase well, the seedlings remaining true to colour since there is little variation in this species. In the same situation, A. ranunculoides can provide a contrast with small, deep yellow flowers, spreading very freely in peaty soil. There are double forms of it and also a hybrid with A. nemorosa – the beautiful pale yellow A. × seemannii. These anemones generally grow to about 6 in. (15 cm) high.

Cyclamen coum (p.47) starts flowering very early and continues well into the spring, to be followed by C. repandum, another shade-loving species with marbled leaves and deep magenta flowers. Recently, a form from southern Greece, 'Pelops', has become more generally available, with paler pink flowers and leaves strikingly spotted with white. C. repandum is a little less hardy than C. coum and this probably applies especially to 'Pelops'. C. libanoticum has the largest, pale pink flowers of all the

Above: *Erythronium revolutum* (left) and E. 'White Beauty' (right) are two robust dog's tooth violets

Below: 'Robinsoniana' is an excellent form of the wood anemone, *A. nemorosa*

Above: A mixture of the blue *Anemone apennina* and its white form
Below: The double form of *A. ranunculoides* (left); *Fritillaria camschat-censis* (right) is one of the species which prefer shade

species. It has acquired an unfortunate reputation for needing cold greenhouse treatment, whereas in fact it can withstand temperatures lower than 0°F (– 18°C). It too does best in partial shade. Although the majority of fritillaries require hot dry conditions, there are some which need shade, humus and moisture to thrive. Into this category fall the uncommon Himalayan species, *Fritillaria cirrhosa*, which has large flowers, either slightly chequered yellow or heavily chequered almost brown, on 8 in. (20 cm) stems, and *F. camschatcensis*, an intriguing plant native to eastern Asia, Alaska and Canada, with nearly black flowers. Another American species and a woodland native is the very variable *F. lanceolata*, up to 18 in. (45 cm) high with several small, dark-spotted flowers to a stem.

SUN-LOVERS

Most fritillaries enjoy a well-drained soil in full sun and the recent introduction or reintroduction of many species has created tremendous interest in the genus. They display an amazing diversity of shape and size and, although their bell-shaped flowers are frequently in sombre shades of green and brown, there are many with brighter colouring. In this limited space, only those which can be easily grown in the open garden are described, but many rarer species are now available from specialists and present little difficulty in a cold greenhouse or frame. Seed is the ideal method of propagation, but many increase by division or by forming small bulbils.

The native snakeshead, *Fritillaria meleagris*, is the most popular, with beautifully chequered bells in pinkish purple or white; it is easily grown in sun or partial shade and even flourishes in grass. In sunny gardens, *F. pyrenaica* is the most reliable of all, with robust 12 in. (30 cm) stems and flowers which are generally deep chocolate in colour, but may vary from pale greenish yellow through intermediate shades. *F. persica* is very different in appearance, with rosettes of grey-green leaves from which emerge tall spikes of small flowers. These may attain as much as 2½ ft (75 cm) in the robust clone 'Adiyaman', which has deep purple flowers with a grape-like bloom, and forms with pale greenish flowers also occur. This species needs a very sunny place to flower well. *F. montana* (*F. nigra*) and the very closely allied *F. ruthenica* grow up to 12 to 18 in. (30–45 cm) high and have several small, very dark brown chequered flowers to a stem.

The Japanese *Fritillaria verticillata*, bearing 2 ft (60 cm) spikes of small straw-coloured flowers, may take a year or two to

Above: *Fritillaria pyrenaica* (left), easily grown in a sunny spot, and *F. pallidiflora* (right), which is better with a little shade
Below: The large, strikingly coloured bells of *F. michailovskyi* (left); the smaller-flowered *F. uva-vulpis* (right) increases freely

become established and flower well, but tolerates cooler conditions. Two other large-flowered species which prefer some shade are *F. raddeana* and *F. pallidiflora*. The former is like a small version of the crown imperial, *F. imperialis*, with flowers of a beautiful greeny yellow. *F. pallidiflora* is an excellent garden plant, easily raised from seed, with rounded glaucous leaves and unusually large, pale yellow flowers, up to three to a stem.

There are many smaller fritillaries suitable for the rock garden or the front of a well-drained border. One of the most exciting recent introductions from Turkey is *Fritillaria michailovskyi*, only 3 to 4 in. (8–10 cm) high with comparatively large flowers, which are deep chocolate towards the base and bright yellow over the outer third – a spectacular contrast. The same colour contrast is seen in *F. uva-vulpis* (*F. assyriaca*), with much smaller flowers on slightly taller stems. *F. minuta* (*F. carduchorum*) is very distinctive in having abundant glossy green leaves and small brick-red flowers.

There are several dwarf fritillaries some 4 to 8 in. (10–20 cm) high which have greenish flowers, either plain or faintly chequered or shaded. Among them are *Fritillaria involucrata*, the very easily grown *F. pontica*, *F. graeca* subsp. *thessala*, also a good garden plant, the taller *F. messanensis* in various forms and the slightly less robust *F. hermonis* subsp. *amana*.

The genus *Corydalis* contains some excellent sun-loving species, with characteristic, tubular, two-lipped flowers and much-divided foliage. *Corydalis solida* is very easy, increasing freely from the tubers and from seed, and has attractive greyish, ferny leaves and 4 in. (10 cm) spikes of purple flowers. *C. decipiens* and the variety *densiflora* (*C. densiflora*) are almost identical to it. *C. solida* 'George Baker' is a magnificent form (originally introduced under the incorrect name of *C. transsilvanica*), with flowers of an exquisite shade of pinkish terracotta. Although rare, it is hardy and very easy to grow in the garden. *C. caucasica* var. *alba* has pure white flowers and seeds itself around in sun or partial shade. *C. bulbosa* (*C. cava*) is a more robust plant which again increases readily, with purple or white flowers.

The flowering of the chionodoxas, known as glory of the snow, usually overlaps with that of the scillas (p. 177) and indeed the two are closely related and frequently hybridize. Chionodoxas are mostly of similar height, up to 6 in. (15 cm), but differ from *Scilla bifolia* and *S. sibirica* in having more white in the flowers. The commonest species is *C. luciliae*, sometimes offered as the larger *C. gigantea*, which has blue flowers with a clear white centre, except in the pale pink form, 'Rosea'. It increases rapidly both by division and self-seeding. *C. sardensis* is similar but smaller, while

'George Baker' a superb form of *Corydalis solida*, which is hardy and easily cultivated

___

the Cretan *C. nana*, only 2 to 4 in. (5–10 cm) high, is the smallest and most delicate of all.

Puschkinia scilloides is very similar to chionodoxa. It is an excellent garden plant whose white flowers have a conspicuous blue line down the centre of the petals. There is also a beautiful pure white variety.

The grape hyacinths are well-known to every gardener, with their spikes of tightly packed bells with incurving lips, ranging from white, through shades of blue, to an unusual deep, almost black colour. All are easily grown; indeed several can become a nuisance, forming myriads of small bulbils which are spread around by digging, and these are only suitable for wilder parts of the garden. Names to beware of in this respect are *Muscari racemosum* and *M. neglectum*, probably synonymous and referring to plants with dense, dark blue, white-rimmed flowers.

Of the many species, varying only in colour, *Muscari azureum*, with clear blue flowers, darker towards the base of the spike, and *M. armenaicum*, with pale blue white-tipped flowers, are the most frequently offered. The tassel hyacinth, *M. comosum*, is much taller, up to 12 in. (30 cm), and has scattered straw-coloured flowers at the base of the spike with densely packed, dark purple flowers above, surmounted by a tassel of paler mauve flowers.

Above: *Corydalis caucascia* (left) delights in sun or some shade; 'Rosea'
(right) a pink form of the versatile *Chionodoxa gigantea*
Below: *Puschkinia scilloides* (left), flowers in very early spring; the odd
feather-duster blooms of *Muscari comosum* 'Plumosum' (right)

Ornithogalum nutans (left) is suitable for naturalizing among shrubs; 'Wisley Blue' (right), an attractive darker form of *Ipheion uniflorum*

This is very easy to grow, but not to everyone's taste. A form known as 'Plumosum' or 'Monstrosum' is sometimes offered, in which all the flowers consist of elongated mauvish tassels.

The genus *Ornithogalum* contains a large number of dwarf species, usually very low-growing and having heads of white flowers with some green markings, but few are in general cultivation. The commonest is *Ornithogalum umbellatum*, the star of Bethlehem, one of the taller species with 6 to 8 in. (15–20 cm) stems bearing several starry white flowers and easily grown in sun or partial shade. *O. nutans* is similar in height, but the large flowers have an intriguing silvery appearance with a grey green backing to the petals. When established, it increases very freely and is perhaps best among shrubs rather than among more delicate plants. The numerous smaller species are all easy to grow in well-drained soil in full sun.

Ipheion uniflorum (*Triteleia uniflora*) is an undemanding plant which thrives in most soils. It has a cluster of narrow leaves and 6 in. (15 cm) stems, each carrying a large, very pale lavender flower with a deeper line down the centre of the petals. 'Wisley Blue' has flowers of a much deeper blue and the recently available 'Froyle Mill' produces even darker flowers, but possibly has a less robust constitution.

Dwarf Bulbs for Summer

By early May, the main flush of bulbs is over, although a few late flowers may still be seen, especially on the tulips, with the brilliant *T. sprengeri* (p. 170) still to come as an afterthought. There are, however, several dwarf bulbs which flower in the summer months, from May to August. Some of them are easily grown plants, while others are on the borderline of hardiness, but worth trying outside in the southern counties.

The alliums or onions contribute a number of hardy bulbous species flowering at some time during the summer. All have globular umbels of flowers, arranged like umbrella spokes, and most smell of onions when crushed. Many excellent plants are too tall to mention here, but *Allium pulchellum* can just be considered, with stems 8 to 10 in. (20–25 cm) high, having rounded heads of pink or white flowers, the lower pendant and the upper upright. Very easy and seeding itself freely, this is one of the best onions to grow in sun or light shade. The similar *A. flavum* is generally a little smaller, with yellow flowers, and varies considerably, the shortest forms, about 4 to 6 in. (10–15 cm) high, being classed as 'Nanum', 'Pumilum' or 'Minus'. In the best varieties, the stems have a noticeable grey bloom which enhances their beauty. The dependable *A. moly* has broad heads of larger yellow flowers on

The dwarf form of the variable *Allium flavum* is a useful plant for the rock garden

Above: *Triteleia laxa* (left) is very hardy and reliable; *T. ixioides* (right) should succeed in a warm position
Below: *Anomatheca laxa* (left) is the only species which can be tried outside; 'Dawn' (right) a form of the tiny *Rhodohypoxis baurii*, provides a long succession of pink flowers

8 in. (20 cm) stems, but makes bulbils excessively and should only be used where it can naturalize unhindered.

One of the best blue-flowered species, *Allium caeruleum* is small enough to be suitable for the rock garden. Most of the smaller species, up to some 10 in. (25 cm) high, have flowers in shades of pink or lavender, among the finest being *A. acuminatum*, and *A. murrayanum*, the latter probably a larger-flowered version of *A. unifolium*. Although the leaves of alliums are often narrow and inconspicuous, in two species they are an important feature. *A. karataviense* has very broad purple-backed leaves and large round heads of pinkish flowers. It is easily grown and worth planting for the leaves alone. *A. akaka* has slightly smaller leaves without the purple tinge, but the large flowerheads are usually a better pink or greenish white colour. It needs a warm position.

Brodiaea and *Triteleia* are two closely related American genera, producing allium-like flowers from late spring to early summer. Many brodiaeas, as they are usually called in nursery lists, belong correctly to *Triteleia*. Although not widely grown, some species are easy and relatively hardy and are useful for contributing shades of blue among shrubs, where that colour is often lacking. *Triteleia laxa (Brodiaea laxa)* is an excellent garden plant which has proved hardy down to 0°F (– 18°C) and which increases and seeds itself freely. It has loose umbels of pale lavender flowers on stems up to 12 in. (30 cm) high. *B. elegans* and *T. bridgesii (B. bridgesii)* are lower-growing, with flowers of a good deep colour.

In addition to these and several other blue-flowered species offered occasionally under *Brodiaea* or *Triteleia*, there are two fine yellow-flowered plants – *Triteleia ixioides (Brodiaea lutea)* and *T. crocea (B. crocea)*, Both have loose heads of yellow flowers, usually with a dark stripe down the centre of each petal, and are hardy in a sunny sheltered place.

Zigadenus is another American genus not often seen in gardens. Two bulbous species sometimes available are *Zigadenus fremontii* and *Z. micranthus*. The leaves appear early in the autumn, but flowering does not usually start until the end of April or later. The flower spikes, 6 to 8 in. (15–20 cm) high, carry a dozen or more small, pale yellow flowers with greenish centres, considerably larger in *Z. fremontii*. They are hardy, at least in the south.

The most spectacular American bulbs are in the genus *Calochortus*, but they are only obtainable from a few specialists and most need to be grown in a greenhouse or frame. The two species most likely to succeed in a warm well-drained position in

'Albrighton', another beautiful selection of *Rhodohypoxis baurii*

the garden are *Calochortus uniflorus* (*C. lilacinus*), with cup-shaped lilac flowers, and *C. venustus*, generally having large, creamy white or yellow flowers with a dark red central blotch.

Habranthus tubispathus (*H. andersonii, Zephyranthes andersonii*) from South America is extremely easy under glass and will survive all but the hardest winters outside. It has bright orange flowers streaked with brown on the outside of the petals, resembling a miniature hippeastrum, to which *Habranthus* are closely allied. These are usually produced in June or July. It seeds itself freely.

Flowering at the same time, the African *Anomatheca laxa* (*Lapeirousia cruenta*) is equally easy in a cool greenhouse and hardy enough to be grown outside in the south. The 6 to 8 in. (15–20 cm) slender stems bear several small, reddish pink flowers with deep red markings towards the base. It sets abundant bright red seeds and sows itself readily under glass. The variety *albus* has pure white flowers.

The South African *Rhodohypoxis* are also hardy in sheltered gardens, but they require a more peaty soil and should not be allowed to dry out completely. They are fascinating plants, ideal for a trough or rock garden, or for pots under glass, since they grow only 2 in. (5 cm) high or less and produce plentiful flowers in shades of pink, red or white, during May and June.

The first species to be introduced was *Rhodohypoxis baurii*, with red or pink flowers, together with the white or very pale variety *platypetala*. From these a number of selections have been made, such as 'Great Scot' and 'Douglas', red, 'Dawn', 'Stella' and 'Fred Broome', pink, and 'Ruth', white. The larger-flowered 'Tetraploid Red' and 'Tetraploid White' are sometimes offered too. The very hardy and freely increasing *R. milloides* is occasionally available and has deep magenta flowers.

The beautiful *Erythronium oregonum* thrives in semi-shade

Gardening
in Ornamental
Containers

RAY WAITE

This patio garden is a good example of how to make a small
space attractive with stone, water, walls and pots

Introduction

Vases, urns, troughs and other ornamental pots have been an important part of gardens for hundreds of years, often enhancing the overall effect in their own right. But never before has container gardening been practised on such a large scale as it is today. Permanent plantings of trees, shrubs and conifers in purpose-built receptacles have become a feature of our town and city centres, while tubs and troughs of seasonal bedding decorate traffic islands and paved public areas. The modern domestic garden, ever shrinking in size, is invariably transformed into a patio and furnished with all sorts of plants in containers. Even people without gardens can resort to window boxes and hanging baskets for a colourful display and these are increasingly popular.

This book is intended to show what can be achieved by 'gardening without a garden'—using containers outside. It describes the various types of container available, including the conventional ones and the more unusual or unexpected, and also suggests do-it-yourself ideas for constructing containers cheaply. General advice is given on cultivation and propagation. This is followed by a list of recommended plants for both seasonal and permanent schemes, with details of their flowering times, hardiness, special needs and suitability for particular situations.

Left: A hanging basket overflowing with trailing and upright fuchsias, pelargoniums and a touch of pale yellow from the petunias
Below: An old farm cart transformed into an eye-catching container

— Conventional Types of Container —

VASES, URNS, POTS AND JARDINIERES

Traditional natural materials like stone and clay will give the most pleasing effect, although the modern alternatives of plastic and glass fibre can be very acceptable if treated sympathetically. There is a wide range of styles and sizes available, at different prices. When choosing a container, one should ensure it matches or associates well with its surroundings, especially paving and walling, and one often finds that a vase or urn with simple lines will fit in best.

Always check that the container has sufficient room for planting and a reasonable depth for the growing medium, especially at the edges, as excessive drying out can be a problem. A minimum depth of 4in. (10cm) at the edges is recommended. It is also wiser to avoid a container with a narrow mouth, because this gives little width at the rim and can be difficult to plant.

Provision for drainage is important and there should be one good-sized hole, or several, in the base. A large hole will need covering with a piece of old clay flower pot, concave side downwards. For smaller holes, broken brick or stones will allow for free drainage. It is a good idea to raise the container on bricks or blocks so that the water can run away, but make sure that it is stable.

Terracotta containers, except the frost-resistant types, may be damaged by frost in winter and should be kept dry and under cover. Even the dry shelter of a hedge or evergreen tree gives good protection and, if the containers can be emptied first, so much the better.

TROUGHS, TUBS AND IMPROVISED PLANTERS

These containers are made from similar materials and some of the plastic and glass fibre models are extremely good. Wood also plays a part and lead is used by at least one manufacturer who has faithfully copied the design and finish of traditional containers. It is still possible to find specialist craftsmen working with metal.

Properly coopered wooden half-barrels or tubs are becoming more difficult to obtain and are quite expensive. If they are to be stored for any length of time, it is worth keeping them wet. This swells the wood and prevents individual slats falling apart. The interior should be charred to reduce rotting, a blow-lamp being the easiest method of doing this. Unseasoned wood should be treated with preservative, using only products recommended for applying to wooden greenhouses and avoiding those like creosote which would harm the plants.

Large planters may be constructed from railway sleepers, fixed together by long coach bolts or large staples at the corners. They can be made to suit a particular space and tiered to give different levels of planting. Beware of splinters and tar. Obviously, all sorts of troughs can be made from wood and painted to match the exterior decoration of the building or other surroundings. Rough sawn wood may be covered in cork bark, which is very weather-resistant.

Bricks, manufactured walling, concrete blocks or stone can be converted into good solid planters. Stone may be made up without cement and sand bonding so that the container can be easily moved or extended as the season or your mood dictates. In this way the gardener can experiment with positioning and size before making a final decision.

Plastic containers can be improvised from various tubs, such as those used to hold putty, and are ideal for small areas. Drainage holes should be made in the bottom and the outside can be painted with 'Snowcem' to give a rough stone-like finish.

WINDOW BOXES

Window boxes are generally used in sunny positions and planted for seasonal display. However, they can also be adapted to permanent planting or, with a suitable range of plants, they can even be placed in quite shady situations. It is interesting to note that the special climate of London, produced by the warmth of the buildings, allows reasonably tender plants to flourish in window boxes and it is not uncommon to see cinerarias, poinsettias, *Solanum capsicastrum* and pot chrysanthemums growing in the open air in winter. Plants of this sort are best plunged in peat in their pots.

Because of their exposed position, window boxes are particularly prone to rapid drying out and watering should always be carried out early and thoroughly. Like other containers, they will need drainage holes, which can be conveniently made in the base at the rear edge. Don't forget that some water is bound to splash down, so be careful about siting anything underneath. (For further notes on watering, see p. 212.)

Proprietary plastic liners are obtainable which help to over-

Above: A variegated hosta in a half-barrel is skilfully repeated in the border beyond and is ideal for a shady situation
Below: A most unexpected receptacle successfully planted with impatiens to demonstrate the many possibilities of container gardening

come the drying problem, or one can cut polythene sheeting to size and lay it inside the box before filling up with potting compost. Several slits should be cut in the bottom of the lining to allow excess water to drain away. Such linings will also prolong the life of wooden window boxes.

It is important to fix window boxes securely. Even the lighter peat-based composts can become quite heavy, especially when saturated with water. One or two brackets underneath the box, secured to the wall with strong screws, provide the most effective support.

The size of window box will inevitably be dictated by the situation, but it is wise to choose as large a one as possible. Generous planting will result in a better display than a single row of plants, while a larger amount of compost will dry out less quickly and allow for better root growth. With larger boxes it is often more convenient to have separate planting units or sections, which will be easy to handle and fairly light to lift if made from wire mesh and lined with polythene. These also enable one to establish the plants in advance and place them in position when in flower.

WALL POTS AND HAY MANGERS

Somewhat akin to window boxes in their effect, both these types of container are widely available.

Clay wall pots are usually designed to be hooked onto a wall and tend to be quite small, roughly equal in size to a 5- or 6-in. (12.5–15cm) pot. They are best devoted to one kind of plant and are particularly effective if several pots are grouped together. However, they may dry out very quickly, especially when exposed to full sun and wind.

Wall pots arranged in a vertical line can be very attractive, but be careful when watering not to let drips damage the flowers in the lower containers. Ideally, the pots should be put on the ground for watering and, once they have drained through, returned to the wall. Plastic wall pots are also obtainable, many of them fitted with a water reservoir.

Genuine hay mangers can still be found in antique shops and at auctions and an enterprising blacksmith will often make one up to order. Their size and scale should be considered in relation to the wall space and also to the setting. In modern surroundings, for instance, the effect could be quite incongruous.

A piece of large meshed chicken netting should be attached to the bars of the manger to hold in the compost. The netting in turn is lined with moss, followed by a sheet of polythene which will help conserve moisture. Sphagnum moss is the best, but is increasingly difficult and expensive to buy. Moreover, it is becoming much less abundant in the wild and every effort should be made to conserve it. Black plastic sheeting on its own is satisfactory, although it looks rather unattractive, especially in the early stages before the plants have grown enough to hide it. Green polythene is not much better.

HANGING BASKETS

Hanging baskets have become extremely popular in recent years. Although traditional wire baskets are still common, the solid plastic kinds are increasingly preferred. These are easy to plant and maintain and often have a water reservoir incorporated, either a saucer clipped on to the basket or as an internal fitment. The hooks and hangers are usually made from plastic and the whole unit is therefore very durable. With their flat bases, these plastic baskets are convenient to work on and can be stood on the greenhouse staging or floor while plants are being established in the early stages. At present they are generally available only in small sizes, but are very effective when planted with a single type of plant.

Wire baskets, on the other hand, can be obtained in various dimensions, some with a galvanized finish and others with a plastic coating. The larger ones, of course, may be planted with an assortment of plants. Being proportionately heavier, they will require stronger brackets or other means of support.

The usual method of planting is to line the basket with moss to retain the potting compost. An additional layer of plastic sheeting can be placed inside the moss to reduce drying out. The basket should be stood on a flower pot of suitable size to keep it upright and steady while planting.

One advantage of a wire basket is that plants can be grown through the sides between the metal strands, which gives a splendid overall display. In this case, it is not practical to include the polythene, since the moss and compost have to be built up in stages. A small amount of moss should be placed in the bottom and covered with a layer of potting compost, in which the first batch of plants is planted round the edge by carefully pushing the root balls between the wires. The roots are then covered with compost, more moss is added at the sides, together with another layer of compost, and the process is repeated until the basket is filled. There should be plenty of moss at the top to make a rim which will retain water and prevent any compost being washed over the edge.

There are several brands of basket liner which can be pur-

202

chased and used instead of moss. One sort made of foam plastic is particularly good. It is a flat disc in which slits are cut from the perimeter towards the centre, thus allowing it to be moulded to the shape of the basket. The plant roots are then gently squeezed through the vertical gaps.

Similar liners are also made from strong impregnated cardboard or compressed fibre. Holes may be cut in the sides with an old apple corer or other tool so that the root systems can be pushed through.

Square wooden baskets, consisting of small slats of a durable wood such as teak, are still in common use for growing certain greenhouse orchids and tree-dwelling plants.

A decorative wooden hanging basket with ivy-leaf pelargonium and the delightful trailing bellflower *Campanula isophylla*

Unusual Containers

The gardener's ingenuity can be a great asset when it comes to finding or making containers and virtually anything that will hold compost and has some provision for drainage can be adapted.

WHEELBARROWS

Wooden wheelbarrows make large containers which are especially suitable for seasonal bedding and those with wooden or well-disguised metal wheels always seem to look best. Traditionally, English elm is the timber employed in the main part of the barrow, being long lasting even when saturated with water. Other woods should be treated with a preservative, if a natural colour is preferred, or may be painted. There are also smaller, less robust wheelbarrows on the market.

HOLLOW LOGS

These make attractive containers and once again elm is the most durable wood for the purpose. Large diameter sections cut in lengths of about 1 foot (30cm) give an ample planting depth for most plants. Any rotting wood should be removed and the inside cleaned back to the solid wood, which is then charred in the same way as a tub (see p. 199). Logs can be arranged at different heights to create a pleasing group.

CHIMNEY POTS

Clay chimney pots vary in size, design and colour and can be an effective feature on a patio or terrace. Although becoming difficult to find, and therefore expensive, they are well worth searching for in builders' yards and on demolition sites. Their small diameter can be a disadvantage, limiting the choice of plants, and a group of at least three pots may give a better display. Large glazed or unglazed drainpipes can be used in the same way.

Chimney pots or pipes should be partly filled with pebbles, gravel or builders' ballast. They can be lined with polythene, with holes cut in the bottom, to reduce drying out.

Left: A small wooden wheelbarrow painted to match its surroundings and burgeoning with African and French marigolds.
Right: An old tree stump hollowed out and planted with zonal pelargonium and *Calocephalus brownii*, together with lobelia and ivy at the side and base

SHELLS

Although they might seem rather alien to the modern garden, large clam-type shells were very much in vogue during Victorian times and earlier. When grottoes were fashionable, shells were used either as decoration or more functionally in association with a cascade of water. They can provide an interesting container for small plants, such as pansies, polyanthus and primroses for spring flowering, followed by *Impatiens* and *Mimulus* in summer. Drainage is difficult because it is almost impossible to drill holes, but if the shell is tilted foward slightly, much of the excess water collected will seep out.

SINKS

Stone sinks, also from bygone days, are ideal for small alpines. One can achieve complete planting schems in miniature and grow a wide selection of plant gems in a group of sinks.

Above: Cool colours in an elegant handmade terracotta pot; white argyranthemums and petunias combine with verbenas and *Helichrysum petiolare*
Below: A litter bin completely covered with *Begonia semperflorens*—an effective use of an otherwise ugly container

A modern glazed sink can also be treated to make an extremely good hewn stone imitation. After removing any pieces of waste pipe left behind, the exterior glazing should be scored to give a key for the initial coating of adhesive. To this is applied the imitation stone covering called hypertufa, made up of equal parts of peat, builder's sand and cement, which should be kneaded on to the outside, over the rim and down the inside, so that there will be no gap between it and the compost.

The work is best carried out in the autumn to allow a longer period for drying and thus ensure a stronger bond. The sink should be kept in a frost-free place during the process. Once the surfaces have dried, they may be painted two or three times with liquid fertilizer, to produce a more natural appearance and hasten the growth of moss.

CAR TYRES

Unlikely as it may seem, rubber car tyres can be transformed into containers which are perfectly acceptable when covered with plant growth. Painted with plastic emulsion paint (PEP), they can be used singly or stacked on top of each other to give a suitable depth of compost. Plants should be placed between the tyres as they are stacked and the compost filled in around the root. The tyres will have a long and useful life, although obviously they will not be easy to move once planted.

LITTER BASKETS

Wire litter baskets of the type seen in car parks have great potential. Taller baskets 3ft (1m) or more high can be used as a free-standing feature, while the smaller waste-paper kind may be turned into a large hanging basket. Alternatively, one can make a cylindrical basket by driving thin stakes into the ground or fixing them to a base and securing chicken netting to them. In this way the diameter and height can be chosen to suit the situation.

Taller containers may need to be stabilized by means of a pipe or stake, which is driven down the centre and into the ground underneath. In addition, a piece of plastic pipe should be inserted in the centre of the basket. It is cut to roughly two thirds the depth of the container, with a few holes bored in the bottom half, allowing more even penetration when filled with water. A lining of moss will retain the compost in the same way as for a hanging basket. Plants can then be grown round the sides to achieve a massed pillar effect.

— Containers for Special Purposes —

STRAWBERRY POTS

A strawberry pot made of clay is a most attractive container, best described as a large jar with holes in the sides. Each hole is of sufficient size to take a strawberry root system and is made with a cupped lower lip to retain compost and water. Once filled with compost, these pots become very heavy and somewhat unwieldy so are best planted up *in situ*. They are now quite expensive, especially those made of frost-resistant clay, but can look very charming, especially when used for flowering plants such as busy lizzies and fibrous-rooted begonias.

A tower of plastic strawberry pots planted with impatiens and, perhaps inadvisedly, topped with pansies

There are also smaller versions for growing herbs. Thyme, marjoram and hyssop are ideal and can be planted together in one pot. Parsley pots are based on the same principle. Two kinds of plastic strawberry planter are on the market. One is quite large and mounted on a small wooden platform fitted with castors, which allows the container to be turned so that all the developing plants and fruit have a share of direct sunlight. (The idea can be similarly adapted for clay pots.) It is possible to make a large planter from a plastic dustbin with holes cut in the sides, or a strong polythene bag. All these sizeable containers need a length of perforated pipe or a core of chicken netting inserted down the centre for watering purposes.

The other type of planter commonly available is much smaller in diameter and comprises a tower made up of sections with cupped holes.

BULB POTS AND BOWLS

Bulb pots of clay or plastic are shaped like miniature squat Ali Baba jars with holes in the sides. The bulbs are placed inside the holes and held in position as the pot is filled with compost. Crocuses are particularly effective when grown in them and grape hyacinths and scillas can also be recommended.

Bulb bowls do not have drainage holes and it is therefore important to use bulb fibre or a similar very open growing medium.

Both these types of container are more often seen indoors, but they can be used quite successfully outside.

GROWING BAGS

The concept of growing bags is totally different to that of all the containers previously discussed, but they merit a mention here because of their importance and popularity. The plastic bags containing the compost tend to be rather garish in colour and, while this does not matter in a greenhouse, they may be somewhat conspicuous in a conservatory or on a patio. Canes pushed into the compost require firm support, which can be achieved by an overhead wire or, where this is not possible or desirable, by a proprietary framework fixing the canes securely at the base.

Growing bags are deservedly popular for several reasons. They contain a sterile and consistent compost which is easy to handle; they can be used in many situations and make the annual preparation, replacement or sterilization of greenhouse borders unnecessary; and they can take a primary crop such as tomatoes, followed

A growing bag newly planted with bedding plants—a practical if not the most decorative container

by a secondary crop like winter lettuce, after which the compost can be used in the garden as a source of humus. Many gardeners find the mini-size growing bags especially convenient.

RING CULTURE POTS

This system, traditionally applied to growing tomatoes, has been largely superseded by the more convenient growing bag, but some gardeners still prefer it. In brief, the method consists of standing a bottomless cardboard pot on clean ash, sand or ballast and filling it with compost. The roots grow through the bottom of the pot into the lower layer, which is kept well watered, and liquid feed is applied directly to the growing medium in the container.

SELF-WATERING CONTAINERS

Now widely used for indoor display, self-watering containers can also be used outside. They are helpful when plants are likely to be left unattended for any length of time, although they are relatively expensive. They come in various shapes, sizes and finishes. The basic principle is that the planter is fitted with a reservoir from which the water rises to the compost above by means of wicks. A small float is connected to a marker at the top of the rim and indicates the amount of water in reserve.

— Management and Maintenance —

THE GROWING MEDIUM

The kind of growing medium required will depend very much on the plant and its situation.

For permanent planting out of doors, plants will do best in a loam-based compost. Good drainage is essential and can be provided by filling the base of the container to a depth of several inches with broken brick, old rubble, large stones etc. Ideally, chopped-up turf should be placed on top of the drainage material before adding the compost, but coarse peat sievings or well-rotted manure are an acceptable alternative. Containers should be filled to the brim with compost and well firmed during the process, allowing some space at the top for watering.

Some settling of the compost is inevitable in the first year, but try to prevent excessive sinking as this looks ugly and deprives the roots of compost. If possible, large containers should be filled well before planting to allow the compost to settle first.

The John Innes formula is still the best for a loam-based compost. JI no. 3 mixture, which contains more fertilizer than JI no. 2, is recommended for vigorous plants. It may be bought ready-made or alternatively prepared at home, by mixing 7 parts by volume of sterilised loam with 3 parts of peat and 2 parts of grit or coarse sand (be sure to use coarse sand and not the finer type), to which is added a balanced fertilizer to keep the plants growing for several weeks. An increased amount of loam will be beneficial for larger containers in which trees and shrubs are to be established.

When a lighter compost is required, for example in hanging baskets or window boxes, a peat-based kind should be chosen. There are many commercial brands available, but for gardeners who wish to mix their own a good general formula is 3 parts by volume of moss peat to one part of coarse sand, with a base fertilizer added in quantities recommended by the manufacturer. Proprietary peat-based composts contain less nutrients and will therefore need feeding sooner.

Always remember to soak peat thoroughly before mixing. Once it has dried out completely (for example on the shelf in a garden centre), it can be difficult to wet properly again. For this reason, some ready-mixed composts contain a wetting agent to facilitate the process. It is also important to ensure that containers do not

211

Clematis macropetala 'Maidwell Hall' in a wine jar, a good example of permanent planting in a large container

dry out when planted up with a peat-based compost. In fact, both loam and peat-based composts benefit from the incorporation of water-retentive polymer granules. These are capable of absorbing and then releasing a large amount of moisture over a long period, at the same time maintaining a good free-draining physical structure to the compost.

WATERING

Lack of water is probably the commonest explanation for dis-appointing results when growing plants in containers. Hanging baskets, wall pots, window boxes, free-standing urns and vases are all particularly vulnerable, especially in hot weather, and may need watering at least once a day. A light breeze can cause serious drying out even in dull weather and, in a densely planted con-tainer, water will simply run off the leaves without soaking the compost after a downpour of rain. Self-watering containers fitted with a small reservoir are obviously helpful, but they are not equipped to keep the compost moist for any length of time.

Planters, window boxes and growing bags can be fitted with irrigation lines. Basically, water comes from nozzles placed at strategic points along a length of tubing which leads back to the water source. The number of nozzles will depend on the size of container and the amount of water required to thoroughly moisten the compost. At the height of sophistication, watering can be automated, although most gardeners will be content to turn on a tap.

Hanging baskets are often difficult to water and a hose may be useful for the purpose. A recent innovation is a hand-held bottle which pumps water up a short lance with a bent top. It is simple and efficient but only satisfactory for dealing with a small number of hanging baskets.

FEEDING

It is not always appreciated that container plants require supplementary feeding and that the compost alone cannot provide sufficient nutrients to maintain good growth after the first two or three weeks. This applies even to containers planted for seasonal display and all the more to long-term planting schemes. One of the simplest methods of feeding is liquid fertilizer, which is easily applied and in a form readily assimilated by the plants. Overall, a mixed fertilizer containing all the essential elements will be the best choice, although a fertilizer with a higher nitrogen content will prove necessary to boost growth and thus prolong flowering.

An alternative is to sprinkle a dry fertilizer on the surface. The resin-coated slow-release type is particularly useful for hanging baskets, while perennial woody plants will benefit from an annual dressing of a general fertilizer.

PROTECTION FROM FROST

Where containers are very close to buildings, they are usually sufficiently protected by the latent heat of the walls and one or two degrees of air frost in late spring will do little harm. However, it is safer to wait until May or June before planting up containers with half-hardy bedding plants. If a late frost is expected, plants can be covered with sheets of newspaper.

In the autumn, it is a wise precaution to take propagating material of tender plants before the threat of severe frosts. A further advantage is that cuttings tend to root quickly in September and the resulting plants will be able to become established for overwintering in a frost-free greenhouse.

In exposed positions, vulnerable subjects such as bay trees

should be moved to a more sheltered part of the garden or placed in a cold greenhouse.

If extra protection is required, hessian or bracken can be used. Both may be supported by means of bamboo canes and kept in place by covering with wire or plastic netting.

PROPAGATION

Seeds

Half-hardy annuals are generally raised from seed sown in heat in February and March. A temperature of about 70° (21°C) suits most of them and after germination the seedlings can be grown on in a cooler temperature of 50 to 60°F (10–16°C). When large enough to handle, they should be pricked out into bigger trays or singly into pots to allow room for development. They should not be planted out until the risk of frost has passed, which may be April or May depending on area. They will require hardening off first to acclimatize them to outdoor conditions and should be moved to a frame or cloche, or placed outside initially for a few hours each day and then for longer periods.

Cuttings

Softwood cuttings are leafy shoots usually taken in the spring when growth is active; semi-hardwood cuttings are riper stems taken later in the season. In both cases they will need some sort of protection, such as a propagating case or frame, to prevent wilting. It is important to select good healthy material from non-flowering growths whenever possible.

September is the best month for autumn propagation and allows the cuttings to become well rooted and established in their pots before the onset of winter. They should be protected from frost.

Silver-foliaged plants should be kept on the dry side, especially when temperatures are low.

Above: Containers grouped on a patio, with pelargonium, impatiens, French marigold, cineraria and a standard fuchsia, and two impressive urns
Below: Half-hardy summer bedding plants—heliotrope, verbena, chrysanthemum, ivy-leaf pelargonium, sweet alyssum—used to good effect

Plants for Outside Containers

The range of plants suitable for growing in containers is enormous, extending far beyond the familiar geraniums, fuchsias and lobelias. Apart from one's own personal preferences, there are many factors dictating the choice of plants.

The most important consideration is the basic nature of the site, whether it is sunny or shaded, sheltered or exposed, which way the walls face and how much space is at one's disposal.

Then, you should think about the type of container for which the plants are destined. Would it look better with a mixture of plants, or a single kind, or just one specimen? What will be the ultimate effect using, say, trailing or bushy plants? And will the plants or the container itself be the main feature?

The actual requirements of the plants are, of course, a priority. Some of the most popular annuals, for instance, need a sunny spot to perform well; and shrubs should be grown in containers which afford plenty of room for their roots. The availability of a greenhouse or some sort of winter protection broadens your scope so that you can include half-hardy and tender plants and also increase stock at home.

In the end, it is a question of the amount of time and money you are prepared to devote to growing plants in containers. If you regard container gardening as a means of achieving a colourful show in the summer, as many people do, you will find it quite labour-intensive. Bedding plants will have to be bought in or raised from seed, and once planted in their containers, will demand constant attention—watering, feeding, deadheading and so on. On the other hand, if you invest in more permanent plants like shrubs and perennials, the initial expense may be greater but the day-to-day maintenance will be less and the results can be enjoyed for several years.

Perhaps the best form of container gardening is a combination of the two approaches, the temporary and the long-term, in which plants are selected both for the seasonal interest of their flowers and for the more lasting contribution of their foliage and shape.

The following list is by no means exhaustive, but gives suggestions for plants that are particularly recommended for growing in containers outside. It includes annuals, perennials and shrubs, arranged under their botanical names in alphabetical order. These are followed by general entries on alpines and bulbs, starting on p. 247.

ABUTILON

A. × hybridum is a tender shrub with chalice-shaped, mallow flowers in shades of orange, salmon or maroon, which appear in early summer and continue right through to the autumn months. It is easily raised from seed from an early March sowing under glass. Cuttings can also be taken to reproduce particular colours, overwintered in frost-free conditions and grown on the following year. It is best used as an accent plant in tubs, urns and planters, as is the heavily variegated form 'Savitzii'. This must be propagated by cuttings and is not hardy.

A. striatum 'Thompsonii' is probably the most popular of all yellow variegated pot plants, further enhanced by its orange flowers. It is capable of making quite large plants fairly quickly and is worth propagating annually by means of cuttings. Although withstanding slight early autumn frosts, it requires winter protection in a frost-free place.

An abutilon lends emphasis to a rich medley of plants, including a bright red verbena, in this handsome urn

AGAPANTHUS

There are many good hybrids of this plant, which is related to the lily. It is particularly fine on its own in large vases or tubs, where its flowers of white or shades of blue above the striking strap-shaped leaves will make a bold display on patios and terraces in late summer and autumn. Although numerous hardy hybrids exist, they cannot be regarded as such when grown in containers, as their roots become vulnerable to extreme cold. They therefore require winter protection. They are increased by division in the spring.

AGAVE AMERICANA

This succulent perennial is another plant needing winter protection. Its stiff rosette of spiny leaves has a sub-tropical air and the yellow- or white-margined forms, *A. americana* var. *marginata*, are particularly effective. The many suckers provide material for easy propagation. They should be removed with a sharp knife and potted singly in small pots, using a sandy compost, in autumn or spring.

AGERATUM HOUSTONIANUM

This very popular annual bedding plant may be raised from seed sown in gentle heat in March. 'Adriatic', 'Blue Blazer' and 'Blue Mink' are all good for edging containers, together with the white forms 'Spindrift' and 'White Cushion'. The taller-growing cultivars 'Blue Bouquet' and 'Tall Blue' mix well with other plants.

The delightful chrysanthemum 'Jamaica Primrose' with petunias, geraniums, mimulus and helichrysum

ANTIRRHINUM MAJUS

The ever-popular **snapdragons** are usually grown as annuals and always give a cheerful show, although they are really only suitable for large containers. They can be sown in January and February in gentle heat and then pricked out and hardened off for planting out in their flowering positions. They may be planted even before the risk of frost has passed. A very wide range of colours and heights is available, some reaching at least 3ft (1m) tall, the dwarf ones hardly exceeding 6in. (15cm). Where antirrhinum rust is prevalent, a few rust-resistant cultivars of medium height can be obtained, although their resistance may not last the whole season.

ARABIS

The pink and white forms of A. *alpina* make good carpeting plants and are easily raised from seed, sown in spring under glass or out of doors in early summer.

A. *blepharophylla* 'Spring Charm' is very compact and has carmine flowers.

ARGYRANTHEMUM

A. *frutescens* (*Chrysanthemum frutescens*), the **Paris daisy** or **marguerite** as it is often known, is widely used in hanging baskets and also in tubs, vases and urns. It can be trained as a standard and underplanted for the summer. It is half-hardy and should be propagated annually in autumn or spring by softwood cuttings. The type with white daisy flowers is most familiar, but there are one or two with cushion-centred pink flowers and feathery grey-green leaves.

A. *leucanthemum* is a hardy perennial with dense yellow flowers, while the cultivar 'Jamaica Primrose' is a paler yellow.

A. *foeniculaceum* is a shrubby **chrysanthemum** with glaucous, much-divided leaves, best grown for foliage effect. (See p. 222.)

ARTEMISIA

A. 'Powis Castle' is a splendid silver foliage plant which can be hardy in favoured positions. However, it is safer to raise new plants each year in autumn from semi-hardwood cuttings and keep them in a frost-free place through the winter.

219

ARUNDINARIA VIRIDISTRIATA

This dwarf **bamboo** has leaves of dark green striped with yellow. It is a most attractive variegated plant, seen at its best in late summer. It is hardy and may be propagated by careful division of the roots in late spring or early autumn.

AUBRIETA DELTOIDEA

Usually seen as a rock plant, this perennial does equally well as an underplanting for spring bulbs. Pink, mauve and blue shades are dominant. It may be propagated by division, cuttings or seed.

BEGONIA

B. pendula is a superb plant for hanging baskets. It requires warmth (75°F; 23°C) to raise from seed, but if tubers are obtained they can be started into growth in the spring in frost-free conditions. There are red, pink and orange cultivars, all giving a good display throughout the summer. The tuberous begonias are excellent for troughs and planters, especially the Non-Stop F_1 hybrids. Propagated from seed sown in heat during early spring, the tubers may be stored over winter and brought into growth again by placing in a seed tray containing peat and keeping in a warm greenhouse or frame.

B. semperflorens, the fibrous-rooted begonia, is deservedly popular. It has a long flowering season and comes in a range of colours from white through pink to red, some cultivars even having bronze leaves. It needs warmth to raise from seed, but most nurserymen have plants available. Advances are continually being made in breeding. The following are particularly recommended for tubs, troughs, window boxes and hanging baskets—'Frilly Pink', 'Frilly Red', 'Pink Avalanche'. (See p. 206.)

None of the bedding begonias are hardy.

BELLIS PERENNIS

The common **daisy** has produced many cultivated forms, large- and small- and double-flowered, in white, pink and red. They flower in spring and summer and, although perennial, are best treated as biennials. They should be sown in boxes or direct into a frame and then either pricked off into boxes or planted out in a nursery plot before moving to their flowering positions in autumn.

BERBERIS

The **barberries**, characterised by their spring growth and yellow flowers in spring, include several useful evergreen shrubs for permanent planting in larger containers. 'Nana', a cultivar of B. *buxifolia*, makes a dense, low mound, while B. *candidula* is a slightly larger dome-shaped bush with bright yellow flowers. 'Irwinii' and 'Corallina Compacta' are two dwarf forms of B. x *stenophylla*.

BRUGMANSIA ARBOREA

This shrub can be raised from seed, although normally grown from cuttings, and ultimately makes a large plant some 5ft (1.5m) or more tall and as wide. Its huge, white, hanging trumpets are very fragrant and give a fine summer display. Plants must be protected from frost and should be cut back hard each spring, shortening the previous year's growth to two buds. It is ideal for a sunny position outside, in a fairly large container. (See p. 222.)

CALCEOLARIA RUGOSA 'SUNSHINE'

This half-hardy plant is happy in sun or light shade and flowers throughout the summer from an early spring sowing under glass. The inflated flower pouches are clear yellow and held on long stems.

CALOCEPHALUS BROWNII

This is a tender shrub of wiry growth covered with dense, white, woolly hairs. Its overall silver appearance and non-rampant growth make it a good filler plant. It should be propagated by cuttings in the autumn. (See p. 205.)

CAMELLIA

The many cultivars of C. *japonica*, one of the hardiest species, are excellent in tubs and pots, except in the north and Scotland where they do not succeed. The C. x *williamsii* varieties are perhaps even better as they tend to be more free-flowering, although more open in habit, and will flower well in the north. The numerous hybrids of C. *reticulata* are also ideal if protected from frost.

Camellias do very well in town gardens and, with their hand-some, evergreen, glossy leaves, are attractive even when not in

221

Above: A superb arrangement of containers and statues on a terrace, dominated by the double form of *Brugmansia arborea* and a stately white lily
Below: The silvery leaves of *Centaurea gymnocarpa* set off the daisy-like flowers of *Argyranthemum foeniculaceum*

Above: *Convolvulus mauritanicus* is ideal for a wide pot or a hanging basket and, although not hardy, is easily increased from cuttings
Below: *Cordyline australis*, sometimes known as cabbage tree, gives a distinctive accent to this mixed planting

flower. They must never be allowed to dry out. They benefit from regular feeding, preferably with a high potash fertilizer (such as a tomato fertilizer) which encourages flowering. (See also the Wisley Handbook *Camellias*.)

CAMPANULA ISOPHYLLA

This trailing **bellflower** is a delightful addition to window boxes and hanging baskets and covers itself with starry blue or white blooms in summer. Sometimes seen as a houseplant, it is not hardy, but may be easily propagated from cuttings. (See p. 203.)

CANNA INDICA

This exotic-looking half-hardy perennial is grown both for foliage and for its showy pink, orange or red flowers. It requires a large container and can be raised from seed. During the winter the fleshy roots should be stored in frost-free conditions and subsequently divided for replanting in late spring.

CENTAUREA GYMNOCARPA

This shrubby plant with silver foliage is slightly tender but easily propagated from seed. Seed-raised plants can be rather coarse and variable in leaf colour. If you have a good form, it is worth keeping it going by taking cuttings in late summer. (See p. 222.)

CHEIRANTHUS

The brilliant orange flowers of the **Siberian wallflower**, *C. × allionii*, appear a little later than those of the ordinary wallflower. It is a shortlived perennial. Seed should be sown outside in midsummer for transplanting in the autumn, or on lighter soils in July and August to avoid premature flowering, the plants being thinned as necessary.

C. cheiri, the true **wallflower**, is still a favourite both for colour and scent. Generally speaking, plain rather than multicoloured kinds look better in a small container. Grown as a biennial, seed is sown outside in midsummer and transplanted into nursery rows, from where the plants are transferred to their flowering positions. Most cultivars grow to about 18in. (50cm), but 'Orange Bedder' and the deep crimson 'Vulcan' are shorter. (See p. 235.)

CHRYSANTHEMUM

See *Argyranthemum.*

CINERARIA

See *Senecio.*

CLEMATIS

The 'queen of climbers' can look very effective grown in a large tub, either trained up wires or netting on a wall, or clambering over a tripod of canes fixed inside the container. (See p. 212.) The tub should be at least 1½ ft (45cm) deep and wide and plentiful watering and a weekly liquid feed will be necessary in the summer. A layer of pebbles on the surface of the compost helps to keep the roots cool. Spring- and early summer-flowering hybrids like the well-known 'Nelly Moser', 'Bees' Jubilee' and 'The President' are useful for north- or east-facing walls; autumn-flowering hybrids such as 'Comtesse de Bouchaud' and 'Jackmanii' prefer a sunny aspect. (See also the Wisley Handbook *Clematis.*)

CONVOLVULUS

C. cneorum, although not entirely hardy, is a small shrub well worth growing for its silvery foliage and trumpet-shaped flowers of white tinged with pink, produced from late spring onwards. Cuttings taken in the summer will root readily in gentle heat.

The beautiful *C. mauritanicus* is slightly trailing and should be propagated by cuttings each autumn to ensure plants for the next summer. (See p. 223.)

CORDYLINE

C. australis and *C. indivisa,* with the sword-like leaves held on a cylindrical stem, are equally impressive whether grown on their own in an urn or vase, or mixed with other plants for emphasis. They are hardy only in favoured areas and winter protection is necessary in most parts of the country. Propagation is from seed sown in warmth in March, which should result in a usable plant within about twelve months. (See p. 223.)

DATURA

See *Brugmansia.*

DIANTHUS

Carnations grown as annuals have become extremely popular and are excellent in containers. Sown in gentle heat in March and then pricked out into small pots or boxes, good-sized plants will come into bloom in June in their final containers and flower throughout the summer and autumn. Among the many forms available are 'Magic Charms' and 'Telstar', both of mixed colours; 'Snow Fire', which has single white flowers with scarlet centres; and the pretty, single-flowered 'Orchid'.

DIMORPHOTHECA

See *Osteospermum*.

DOROTHEANTHUS BELLIDIFORMIS

This tender annual succulent, often known as *Mesembryanthemum criniflorum*, has daisy-like flowers in a wide range of colours and should be grown in a container placed in full sun, without allowing the compost to dry out too much. Seed may be sown under glass in spring and the seedlings pricked out into boxes before being established in their flowering positions.

ELAEAGNUS

Two valuable variegated plants in this genus are *E.* × *ebbingei* 'Gilt Edge', with a gold band to the foliage, and *E. pungens* 'Maculata', which has leaves splashed with rich yellow. Both are large evergreen shrubs and should be grown in a spacious tub or barrel.

EUONYMUS FORTUNEI

'Emerald 'n' Gold' and 'Emerald Gaiety', gold- and silver-variegated respectively, are two excellent hardy evergreen shrubs. They may be allowed to trail or climb and will do equally well in sun or shade. 'Kewensis' is a miniature version with plain green leaves. All can be easily increased from cuttings at almost any time of year.

FATSIA JAPONICA

A familiar house plant, this imposing evergreen is a splendid specimen shrub for an outside container. Its glossy palmate leaves are complemented by white flowers in the autumn and it is perfectly hardy. It may be increased by cuttings taken in late summer. It is very useful for a shady situation.

FELICIA AMELLOIDES

This half-hardy perennial may be propagated by cuttings in autumn or spring. In growth it tends to cascade and bears bright blue daisy-like flowers which continue all summer. There is also a variegated form.

FUCHSIA

These well-known summer-flowering shrubs are grown in all sorts of containers and the pendulous forms are particularly suitable for hanging baskets. There are many cultivars to choose from, including some with variegated or golden foliage. It is important that the plants are kept well-watered and fed during the growing season. During the dormant winter period they should be protected from frost. Softwood cuttings root very readily in the spring. (See also the Wisley Handbook *Fuchsias*.)

Recommended trailing or semi-trailing types include 'Auntie Jinks'; 'Bon Bon'; 'Bouffant'; 'Cascade'; 'Daisy Bell'; 'Golden Marinka' with golden foliage; 'Marinka'; 'Red Spider'; 'Summer Snow'; and 'White Spider'.

Among the bush forms are the compact 'Alice Hoffman'; 'Army Nurse'; 'Charming'; 'Golden Treasure'; 'Leverkusen'; 'Sunray', with variegated leaves; and the dwarf 'Tom Thumb'.

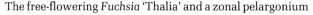

The free-flowering *Fuchsia* 'Thalia' and a zonal pelargonium

A modern container makes a bold display with petunias and the feathery rich green leaves of *Grevillea robusta*

GAZANIA

Grown as a half-hardy annual, this member of the daisy family revels in full sun and to a certain extent withstands dry conditions. Selected forms can only be propagated from cuttings, taken in autumn and spring, although it is more usually raised from seed. Recent strains include Sundance, in shades of scarlet, orange, carmine pink and bronze, and Ministar, yellow and white.

GLECHOMA HEDERACEA 'VARIEGATA'

The variegated **ground ivy**, with white-splashed leaves and long trailing stems, is a good plant for hanging baskets. It is a hardy perennial and should be propagated from cuttings under glass in spring.

GREVILLEA ROBUSTA

This is a perfect accent plant, its decorative ferny leaves providing a wonderful foil for most other plants grown with it. It is a tender shrub and can be difficult to raise from seed. However, plants propagated in the summer will be about 2ft (60cm) high the following spring.

HEDERA HELIX

The common **ivy** and its many forms are invaluable in hanging baskets and, because of their hardiness, can even be left outside in winter. They may be trained into a pyramid or fan or simply allowed to trail over the edge. They need to be trimmed in the spring to keep them tidy. Variegated ivies look particularly well in shady situations and are useful in problem areas such as a north-facing wall or patio. They are readily increased from semi-hardwood cuttings at almost any time of year. (See pp. 230 and 249.)

HEBE

Generally neat and compact in habit, the shrubby **veronicas** produce their panicles of bloom in shades of white, lavender or pink from spring to autumn. They are evergreen and easily grown, although they may suffer in severe winters. Propagation is from cuttings of young wood in the summer. There are numerous garden hybrids available as well as the species.

HELICHRYSUM

H. microphyllum is a small-leaved, silver-grey foliage plant. It is not too rampant and is good for edging or filling a container. Cuttings should be rooted in spring or autumn.

H. petiolare is a much coarser sprawling shrub, with woolly grey leaves. It is often seen as a bedding plant but is excellent in larger containers and hanging baskets. It should be overwintered in a frost-free place. A variegated form is obtainable and also a yellow-leaved sort, 'Sulphureum', sometimes known wrongly as 'Limelight'. Cuttings should be rooted in spring or autumn, as an insurance against loss of the parent plant.

HYDRANGEA

Hortensia and lacecap hydrangeas are often grown in tubs or barrels and their flowers make a welcome contribution in late summer and autumn. There are many other excellent hydrangeas for the purpose, such as the distinctive 'Ayesha', with its lilac-like blooms; *H. paniculata*, with creamy white pyramidal panicles, and its forms 'Grandiflora' and 'Praecox'; and the smaller *H. serrata* 'Grayswood' and 'Preziosa'. All hydrangeas need large containers and should never be allowed to dry out. It is wise to give them some protection in severe winters. Old flowering wood

Above: A hortensia hydrangea with ivy in a terracotta pot—a good combination of two reliable plants for permanent containers
Below: *Ipomoea* 'Flying Saucers' left to scramble around a window box

on hortensias and lacecaps should be removed annually for best effect, while *H. paniculata* requires pruning each spring to one or two pairs of buds from the previous year's growth.

IMPATIENS

Busy lizzies have become extremely popular over the last decade or so and plant breeders are producing numerous cultivars, some with double flowers. They thrive in cool shade and in sun, flowering continuously throughout the summer and autumn until the frosts. Though perennial, they are usually treated as a half-hardy annual. Seed should be germinated at a minimum temperature of 70°F (21°C), in full light and high humidity, enclosing the seed tray in a polythene bag. (See pp. 200 and 208.)

IPOMOEA

The **morning glories** are mostly climbers for training up a trellis in a sunny position. However, the small-growing cultivar 'Minibar Rose' can be encouraged to trail. Its leaves resemble those of a variegated ivy and it bears a profusion of trumpet-shaped flowers, rose-pink edged with white. Germination can be assisted by chipping the seeds (nicking or scratching the hard outer coat) or soaking them in warm water overnight before sowing. It is definitely a half-hardy annual.

LANTANA

In the past it was quite easy to buy seed of *L. camara*, a half-hardy shrub, but it is now stocked by only a very few firms. However, rooted cuttings or established plants of selected colour forms are sometimes available from local nurseries. Although prone to whitefly infestation, it makes an excellent semi-trailing container plants, with dense flowerheads ranging in colour from white, pink, lilac and mauve to orange and red.

L. selloviana is a rosy lilac species which is much more slender in growth but equally decorative.

LATHYRUS

The **sweet pea**, a climbing hardy annual, is a universal favourite. Tall-growing sweet peas are available in a whole range of different shades and do particularly well in growing bags, although troughs, tubs and other containers are quite adequate.

Some support should be provided in the form of string, netting, canes or twiggy sticks. However, the dwarf cultivars, which reach about 3ft (1m) in height, are less likely to need staking or can simply be allowed to cascade. They are good in vases or urns and come in mixed colours, for instance Knee Hi and Jet Set. Seed should be sown in early spring in gentle heat.

LAURUS NOBILIS

The sweet **bay tree**, clipped into a round or oval outline, is the archetypal container plant. It should be pruned to shape during the growing season. Although it is hardy, the foliage tends to be damaged by wind or frost scorch and it should have some winter protection.

LAVANDULA

Among the **lavenders**, the popular 'Hidcote' and the so-called Dutch lavender L. vera, as it is wrongly known, are especially recommended. The first is a compact silvery shrub with dense spikes of violet flowers appearing in early July. The second is somewhat taller and later flowering.

LEUCOPHYTA

See *Calocephalus*.

LILIUM

Some of the most reliable **lilies** for growing in pots and tubs are L. auratum, L. longiflorum, L. speciosum, L. lancifolium (L. tigrinum) and the hybrid 'Enchantment'. They need fairly deep containers and a well-drained compost and may be planted individually in 6 to 7½in. (15–20cm) pots or several together in a larger tub. The bulbs should be potted in spring and stood in a cold frame or in the shelter of a wall or hedge. It is advisable to cover the surface with a layer of peat or leaf mould and to give little or no water until the roots have developed and the shoots are emerging. The pots may then be moved to their summer positions, in sun or light shade. (See also the Wisley Handbook Lilies.)

LOBELIA

The trailing lobelia, L. erinus, is an ever-popular hanging basket plant, with many cultivars available including 'Light Blue Basket',

Blue lobelia is one of the most worthwhile plants for hanging baskets

'Blue Basket' and 'Red Cascade'. The compact edging types can be used to good effect in other containers. In this category 'Cambridge Blue' and 'Crystal Palace', with dark foliage and deep blue flowers, and 'Rosamond', crimson-flowered with a white eye, are all satisfactory. A half-hardy perennial generally grown as an annual, it is propagated by seed sown in gentle heat during February and March.

L. valida is a much stronger growing species than *L. erinus* and may be raised from seed or cuttings. Its clear blue flowers with a distinct white centre blend particularly well with other plants and it deserves to be more widely grown.

LOBULARIA MARITIMA

Sweet alyssum is a well-known edger and, although a true hardy annual, it is better raised as a half-hardy, sown under glass in late March to April. As well as the familiar white forms like 'Snowdrift' and 'Carpet of Snow', there are several attractive coloured forms, such as the rich purple 'Oriental Night', lilac pink 'Rosie O' Day', purple 'Royal Carpet' and red purple 'Wonderland'.

MESEMBRYANTHEMUM

See *Dorotheanthus*.

MIMULUS MOSCHATUS

With recent developments in plant breeding, there are now a number of F_1 hybrids on the market, including 'Royal Velvet', mahogany red with a spotted golden throat; 'Malibu Orange'; and 'Calipso Mixed'. The **musk** is a hardy perennial and should be kept well watered, which will ensure a long flowering season. Seed is sown under glass in early spring.

MYOSOTIS SYLVATICA

The biennial **forget-me-not** is an old favourite for spring flowers. Seed should be sown outside in the summer and the plants grown on in nursery rows before transferring to their final positions in containers. 'Blue Ball', 'Blue Banquet' and 'Royal Blue' are the best among the various shades of blue. 'Carmine King' and 'Rose Pink' are examples of other colours and there is also a white form, although it is not outstanding.

Above: A well known but charming combination of forget-me-nots and dwarf wallflowers in a half-barrel
Below: Nicotiana Nicki Mixture and lobelia make a fine display in a permanent brick container

NEMESIA STRUMOSA

This brightly coloured half-hardy annual is an ideal plant for containers. Seeds should be sown in heat in March and the seedlings pricked out into boxes for hardening off, before planting when the risk of frosts has passed. Carnival Mixture is the best for general purposes, bearing large flowers on compact plants, while 'Blue Gem' is more slender in growth and intermingles well.

NICOTIANA AFFINIS

The **tobacco plant**, with its scented white flowers, grows to a height of about 3ft (1m) and is therefore only suitable for large containers. However, hybridists have made great advances, resulting in short compact plants with upward-facing flowers which open in the day. Unfortunately, the perfume has been diminished in the process, except in the taller forms like 'Evening Fragrance', coming in a mixture of pink, red, mauve, purple and white. 'Domino Mixed' grows to 1ft (30cm) high and Nicki Mixture to only 10in. (25cm), both covering a good range of colours including lime green. Seed of this half-hardy annual may be sown under glass as late as April. (See p. 235.)

OSTEOSPERMUM

This group of daisy-like annuals and perennials includes *Dimorphotheca*, which is the more usual name for those annuals raised from seed, such as *D. aurantiaca* 'Glistening White' and 'Giant Orange'.

Of the perennial *Osteospermum* there are some excellent named cultivars, including 'Blue Streak', white and blue; 'Buttermilk', yellow; 'Tresco Purple', purple, low-growing; 'Whirligig', white, with spoon-shaped petals showing the reverse side of blue. All these are half-hardy and require full sun to perform well. They are best overwintered as young plants raised from cuttings, which should be taken in late summer.

PELARGONIUM

The **geraniums**, as they are commonly known, need no introduction. They revel in sunny positions and, although they can withstand a certain amount of dryness, they need to be kept properly watered and fed to give of their best.

The ivy-leaved geraniums, with their slender stems and tendency to trail, are perfect in hanging baskets and for edging window boxes and containers. (See p. 203.) Recommended cultivars are 'Ailsa Garland', deep pink; 'Blue Spring', with shorter trailing growths and mauve-purple flowers; 'Crocodile', pink with cream-netted variegation; 'Galilee', rose-pink; 'Mme Crousse', pale pink; 'Rouletta', white flowers with red streaks; 'Scarlet Crousse'; 'Snowdrift'; 'Tania' and 'Yale', light and deep crimson; and 'White Mesh', gold-netted variegation on the leaves and rose-pink flowers. Some very profuse-flowering kinds have been introduced recently from the Continent and are becoming more widely available.

The traditional zonal pelargoniums are equally at home in a variety of containers and, like the ivy-leaved ones, flower throughout the summer and on into early autumn. Among the single-flowered kinds are the orange-red 'Maxim Kovaleski' and scarlet 'Paul Crampel'. Double-flowered cultivars include 'A.A. Mayne', magenta; 'Double Henry Jacoby', bright red; 'Gustav Emich', scarlet; 'Hermine', white; 'King of Denmark', salmon-pink; 'Mrs Lawrence', clear pink; 'Orangesonne', brilliant orange; and 'Ted Brook', purple. Zonals that may be raised from seed are 'Cherry Diamond', vivid red; 'Hollywood Star', rose-pink and white; 'Orbit White'; and 'Scarlet Diamond'. (See pp. 205 and 227.)

Variegated and coloured-leaf geraniums are very attractive, although the flowers may be relatively insignificant. A selection of cultivars is 'Caroline Schmidt', silver with bright red double flowers; 'Chelsea Gem', silver and pink; 'Crystal Palace Gem', yellow leaves with green markings and rose flowers; 'Dolly Varden', tricolor foliage of cream, rosy red and green with red flowers; 'Flower of Spring', silver with single scarlet flowers; 'Frank Headley', small silver leaves and salmon flowers; 'Golden Harry Hieover', with a chestnut zone on golden green leaves and red flowers; 'Happy Thought', yellow butterfly patches on bright green with rose flowers; 'Lady Plymouth', cream and green variegation; 'Mrs Parker', silver and rose-pink; 'Mrs Pollock', golden tricolor with orange-red flowers; and 'Mrs Quilter', bronze and pink.

Over the past decade, hybridists have made great progress in developing seed-raised strains of the zonal pelargoniums and even the ivy-leaved geranium is now receiving their attention. Seed can be sown in autumn or spring, when a temperature of 74°F (23°C) should be maintained to ensure good germination.

Ideally the seedlings should be grown on in a temperature of 60°
to 65°F (16°–18°C). However, many gardeners still prefer to
propagate from cuttings as it can be expensive to provide the
necessary warmth to bring young seed-raised plants through the
winter. (See also the Wisley Handbook *Pelargoniums*.)

PERILLA FRUTESCENS

This is a fine purple-leaved plant attaining about 2ft (60cm) in
height, which is best used as an accent plant in larger con-
tainers.The forms *nankinensis* and *laciniata* are very ornamental
with their curly-edged and deeply cut leaves. It is a half-hardy
annual, raised from seed sown under glass in the spring. The
flowers are relatively insignificant.

A splendid mass of petunias concealing the container

PETUNIA

Deservedly popular for all sorts of containers, petunia cultivars are available in a quite bewildering number. They range in height and also in colour, through white, yellow, pink, red, blue and purple, together with striped and bicolors. Recent introductions include strains which are less susceptible to damage from rain. Seed of this half-hardy annual is sown in gentle heat under glass in spring and should be left uncovered to ensure good germination. (See also p. 228.)

PHORMIUM TENAX

This is an exotic evergreen foliage plant with long sword-like leaves, suitable for a large container. Some of the more recently introduced types with striking variegation are of doubtful hardiness, but all are tolerant of a wide range of conditions.

POLYGONUM CAPITATUM

This half-hardy perennial is a good trailing plant for hanging baskets and other containers in a sheltered spot. The zoned evergreen leaves and small pink globular heads of flower remain attractive throughout the growing season. Seed should be sown in March under glass.

PORTULACA

Grown as a half-hardy annual, this makes a nice edging plant for a small container in full sun, with richly coloured flowers of rose, orange, rosy purple, yellow or white. The double forms, although expensive, are the most easily obtainable and of these 'Sunglo' is by far the best. Seed should be sown under glass in March.

PRIMULA

The **polyanthus** is the most useful representative of this large genus for growing in a container and one of the finest of all the spring-flowering plants. There are many good strains available. Seed may be sown in heat under glass in January or February or in a cold frame in April or May. The seedlings should be pricked off into boxes and subsequently planted in nursery rows, before moving to their flowering positions in containers. After flowering the best plants can be retained by lifting them, splitting down to single crowns and planting in a reserve bed. (See p. 206.)

239

Rhododendron 'Madam Masson', perfect for brightening the corner of a terrace or a similar shady spot

RHODODENDRON

Most rhododendrons are potential container plants, given a large enough tub. Gardeners with chalky or limy soil, where rhododendrons rarely succeed, will also find this a useful method. Rhododendrons require a lime-free compost (for instance, Arthur Bower's ericaceous) and plentiful watering. The beautiful hybrids of the dwarf R. *yakushimanum*, producing their abundant flowers in a range of colours in May and June, are particularly worthwhile. (See also the Wisley Handbook *Rhododendrons*.)

RICINUS COMMUNIS

The true **castor oil plant** is an elegant tropical shrub, usually treated as a half-hardy annual. The bold palmate leaves and conspicuous spiny fruits are very impressive in a large mixed display of plants or when several are grouped alone in a single container. Two forms, 'Gibsonii' and 'Impala', have bronze-red leaves, the latter with particularly striking flowers and fruits. The variety *zanzibarensis* has very large, bright green, veined leaves up to 2ft (60cm) across. They are readily raised from seed sown under glass in spring.

SALPIGLOSSIS SINUATA

This is one of the most beautiful half-hardy annuals, with large trumpet-shaped flowers in various colours and often patterned or striped. 'Bolero' and 'Flash' are two very good recent introductions. From a spring sowing under glass, plants will grow to about 2ft (60cm). However, much stronger specimens will result from an autumn sowing, needing just frost-free conditions to keep them going through the winter, and will flower in May and June.

SALVIA

The common **sage**, *S. officinalis*, with its felted grey aromatic leaves, has been cultivated as a herb for centuries. It is also an ideal small hardy shrub for containers, particularly in the variegated version, 'Icterina', and the purple-leaved form, 'Purpurascens'. It is readily increased from cuttings in the sumer.

Generally grown as a half-hardy annual, *S. farinacea* is a fairly vigorous plant and can be useful for its upright habit. The cultivar 'Victoria' carries dense spikes of violet blue flowers. Seed sown in March under glass will result in plants ready for planting out in the south by the beginning of June.

There is probably no better red flowering plant for summer display than the familiar *S. splendens*. Among a number of cultivars, 'Carabinière', 'Red Hussar', 'Red Silver' and 'Royal Mountie' can be recommended. Seed sown in early spring requires temperatures of 68°F (18°C) to germinate freely and reasonable warmth afterwards to get the plants growing away strongly. Although it is preferable to raise them singly in pots, plants can be successful in trays so long as the roots do not

241

become too box-bound. Rose, pink, purple and white forms can also be found, though usually in seedsmen's mixtures.

SEDUM SPECTABILE

This autumn-flowering perennial succulent is perfect for a hot, dry situation. Although it will, of course, require watering in a container, it can survive periods of drought without ill effect. The cool green foliage is handsome throughout the summer, followed by flat flowerheads of pink which attract butterflies. 'Autumn Joy' has bright rose flowers and purplish stems, while 'Brilliant', with bright pink flowers, is one of the best of the **ice plants**.

SENECIO CINERARIA

Often listed as *Cineraria maritima*, this neat silver-grey shrub is half-hardy and should be raised from seed sown under glass.

STENOTAPHRUM SECUNDATUM 'VARIEGATUM'

This tropical creeping ornamental grass with cream-striped leaves is attractive in hanging baskets. It is easily propagated from cuttings at any time.

TAGETES

This generic name embraces the **African** and **French marigolds** and hybrids of the two. Many cultivars have been raised with single, double or crested-centre flowers, in shades of yellow to orange, and ranging in height from 6 to 15in. (15–38cm). They are all invaluable in containers, making a fine display over a long period, and are easy to germinate under glass in spring for growing on and then planting out after the frosts. (See p. 205.)

T. tenuifolia pumila, another half-hardy annual, forms bushy plants which are profusely covered in single flowers. It grows up to 10in. (25cm) high, depending on the cultivar, and is equally easy to raise from seed.

THUNBERGIA ALATA

Black-eyed Susan is a climbing or trailing plant to approximately 3ft (1m) high. It has white, yellow or orange flowers, usually with a black centre, although the cultivar 'Susie' lacks the dark

Thunbergia alata trained into a spectacular column

eye. Grown as a half-hardy annual, it is raised from seed sown under glass in April.

TOLMIEA MENZIESII

Sometimes seen as a house plant, this evergreen perennial is completely hardy and very adaptable, thriving outside in a semi-shaded position. It may be planted on its own in a hanging basket and, although not fully trailing, will soon cover it with heart-shaped leaves, green or variegated. Propagation is by division in autumn to spring or alternatively, in late summer and autumn, by pegging down individual leaves which will form small plantlets at the base—whence the common name pig-a-back plant.

TROPAEOLUM

The gardener's **nasturtium**, *T. majus*, is perfect for pots, baskets and window boxes, although unfortunately prone to attack by blackfly. Double Gleam Hybrids can be recommended for general use and grow to about 15in. (39cm). 'Alaska' is an interesting cultivar with variegated foliage about 1ft (30cm) high, while 'Jewel Mixed' and the dark-leaved, crimson-flowered 'Empress of India' are even dwarfer. All nasturtiums can be sown *in situ* or grown singly in smaller pots for subsequent planting out in containers. A sunny position is important for them to flower well.

T. peregrinum, the **canary creeper**, is a vigorous climber which bears abundant small lemon-yellow flowers in summer. Seed should be sown in April under glass.

VERBENA

Several mixed strains of *V. × hybrida* are on the market, together with single coloured forms in pink, scarlet and violet blue. These are all grown as half-hardy annuals and raised from seed, which at times can prove difficult. Keeping the compost fairly dry will encourage even germination and temperatures of 68° to 78°F (20°–25°C) are recommended. In addition, some excellent named kinds have been selected, which must be propagated by cuttings taken in autumn and spring and require protection from frost in winter. They include 'Lawrence Johnston', crimson; 'Loveliness', mauve-violet; 'Silver Ann' also known as 'Pink Bouquet', strong pink; and 'Sissinghurst', magenta.

Three perennial verbenas are worthy of note. *V. rigida* (*V. venosa*), with purple flowers, is a somewhat stiff plant reaching a height of about 2ft (60cm), and *V. canadensis* (*V. aubletia* of catalogues) has magenta flowers. Both come fairly readily from spring-sown seed. Grown as a half-hardy annual, *V. peruviana* (*V. chamaedrifolia* or *V. chamaedrioides*) is of slender habit, with bright red flowers, and is propagated from cuttings. *V. tenera* 'Mahonettii' is reddish violet with the petals rayed and margined white. It is a slightly weak-growing plant, which needs care in overwintering, and should be propagated by cuttings.

VINCA

The **periwinkles**, *V. major* and *V. minor*, are vigorous trailers which do well in sun or shade. There are several decorative varie-

Above: The unusual variegated nasturtium 'Alaska', with its flowers of many colours, may be grown in a hanging basket or simply allowed to sprawl
Below: Verbena 'Loveliness' mixed with *Felicia amelloides*, helichrysum and centaurea

gated forms and the flowers, usually bright blue, are borne continuously throughout the spring and early summer. They are very easy to propagate from cuttings.

VIOLA

Pansies are invaluable container plants and there have been great advances in breeding, especially with the winter-flowering types. These will flower continuously from the autumn through to spring, depending on the weather, and are ideal not only in pots and window boxes but also in hanging baskets. They are easily raised from seed sown in June or July in trays or prepared beds and then pricked out into boxes or nursery rows. 'Azure Blue', Universal Mixture and Golden Champion are good choices.

Summer-flowering pansies are particularly useful for containers in shaded positions. They include 'Ullswater'; 'Crimson Queen'; Clear Crystals Mixed; and Roggli Giant. They are usually grown as half-hardy annuals, from seed sown in early spring. (See p. 208.)

ZEA MAYS

The variegated **sweetcorn**, with its white- or yellow-and-white striped leaves, is an imposing plant which remains decorative throughout the growing season. It is an annual, easily raised from seed and grown on singly in pots, and will require a fairly large container.

ZINNIA ELEGANS

This half-hardy annual can be obtained in a very wide range of colour, size and shape of flower. The giant-flowered kinds may attain 2ft (60cm) or more, some having quilled petals, others giving a ruffled effect. There are also many fully double and single-flowered sorts, with both large and small blooms. The shorter ones, growing 6 to 12in. (15–20cm) high, make excellent edgers. The young plants resent root disturbance and are best grown on from seedlings in small pots, having been sown in March and germinated at 68°F (20°C). They flower particularly well in hot dry summers.

A trough garden planted with saxifrage and sempervivum, two of the easiest alpines

ALPINES

There are many exquisite gems among the alpines that lend themselves to container growing. One of their main attractions is that such a large number of different species can be grown in a small space and, with careful choice, a permanent miniature garden can be created. Old or simulated stone troughs are ideal, most requiring an open, sunny situation and very sharp drainage. The list below is just a small sample of the many plants suitable for sinks and troughs. (See also the Wisley Handbook *Alpines.*)

Alyssum serpyllifolia—a dense grey mat of leaves with bright yellow flowers in June.
Aquilegia bertolonii—tufts of hairy greyish green foliage and violet-blue columbine flowers in May.
Artemisia assoanum—a prostrate spreading foliage plant with silver leaves.
Asperula caespitosa lilaciflora—a carpet of bright green leaves with tubular, deep carmine blooms in summer.

Campanula arvatica 'Alba'—large white starry flowers borne above bright green leaves in June.

Cyananthus microphyllus—a trailing plant related to campanula, with blue flowers in August; best in a shady position.

Dianthus alpinus—cushion-forming, with fringed carnation flowers of pink and white in June.

Draba aizoides—a hummock of small rigid leaves covered in pale yellow flowers in April.

Dryas octopetala 'Minor'—a creeper with woolly leaves and white flowers followed by fluffy seedheads.

Gentiana verna angulosa—a form of the well-known spring gentian, producing rich blue flowers in April.

Helianthemum alpestre · 'Serpyllifolium'—a prostrate rock rose with abundant yellow saucer-shaped flowers in summer.

Ilex crenata 'Mariesii'—a slow-growing dwarf holly.

Juniperus communis 'Compressa'—a miniature juniper of columnar habit and dense grey-green foliage.

Phlox douglasii 'Crackerjack'—a thick mat with a profusion of crimson-red flowers in early summer.

Potentilla nitida 'Rubra'—large deep rose-pink flowers in July and August above ground-hugging silvery leaves.

Primula marginata forms—easily grown alpines valued for their mealy leaves and delightful scented flowers in various shades of lavender.

Ramonda myconi—a rosette of green leaves and large open flowers of pale blue with yellow centres in early summer; prefers a shady spot.

Salix × boydii—a beautiful dwarf willow with pale yellow catkins in May.

Saxifraga—plants in the Euaizoonia section form rosettes of silvery leaves and bear elegant starry flowers in summer; those in the Engleria and Kabschia sections are smaller and denser, with saucer-shaped blooms; *S. oppositifolia* 'Ruth Draper' is creeping and has cup-shaped flowers of rich red in spring.

Sedum cauticolum—a trailing mat with grey-green leaves and deep purple-red flowers in September.

Sempervivum—the houseleeks, with succulent evergreen leaves in tight rosettes; the cobweb houseleek, *S. arachnoideum*, has the added attraction of bright rose-red flowers in summer and 'Minor' is a choice form.

Sisyrinchium macounianum 'Album'—fans of small leaves like an iris and numerous large white flowers.

Sorbus reducta—a diminutive slow-growing shrub with crimson berries and fine autumn foliage.

BULBS

Spring-flowering bulbs are always welcome for their cheerful colours early in the year and, in many respects, are ideal for containers. They are easily grown, require little attention, except for occasional watering to prevent the compost drying out, and succeed in sun or shade and in a sheltered or exposed position.

However, bulbs have two obvious disadvantages. After planting in the autumn, they do not produce results for several months and the containers remain bare during this time; and, once they have flowered, the leaves start to die down and the plants become untidy. A solution to both these problems is to grow the bulbs in pots and transfer them to the container as they come into bloom, replacing as necessary those which are already over. Alternatively, bulbs can simply be treated as bedding plants, to be planted, enjoyed and then discarded.

Dwarf bulbs are the most practical and rewarding choice for containers and it is wiser to avoid tall-growing daffodils and tulips, as they tend to be damaged by the wind. For maximum effect, the bulbs should be planted in generous groups, rather than regimented rows, and close together (no more than an inch apart).

Mixed daffodils and ivy in a decorative old container

Index

libanoticum 180
mirabile 173
purpurascens 173
repandum 180
rohlfsianum 173
Cytisus 27, 28
battandieri 70, 97, 133
kewensis 28
praecox 28, 48
Daboecia 26
daffodils 138, 143, 145, 249, *249*
daisies, Michaelmas 81
Daphne mezereum 26
odora 'Aureomarginata' 26
Dendromecon rigida 97
Desfontainea spinosa 97, 133
Dianthus alpinus 248
cultivars 226
Digitalis purpurea Excelsior hybrids
57, *57*
Dimorphotheca aurantiaca 236
Doronicum 'Spring Beauty' 42
Dorotheanthus belladiformis 226
Draba aizoides 248
Dryas octopetala 'Minor' 248
Eccremocarpus scaber 98, *104*
Eleagnus × *ebbingei* 'Gilt Edge' 226
pungens 'Dicksonii' 26
'Maculata' 15, 26, *29*, 226
epimediums 13
Eranthis hyemalis 144, 175
Erica 26
herbacea 16, 25
Erythrina cristagalli 98, *101*
Erythronium 142
americanum 180
californicum 180
dens-canis 179
helenae 180
hendersonii 180
oregonum 180, *193*
revolutum 180, *181*
tuolumnense 180
'White Beauty' 180, *181*
Escallonia 133
'Apple Blossom' 30
'Glory of Donard' 30
× *iveyi* 98
eschscholzias 53
Euonymus fortunei 132
'Emerald an' Gold' 31, 226
'Emerald Gaiety' 226
'Silver Queen' 31, 99
var. *radicans* 98
Euphorbia characias 43
wulfenii 50
griffithii 'Fireglow' 43
polychroma 43

robbiae 43
Fabiana imbricata 99
Fatsia japonica 32, *33*, 226
Feijoa sellowiana 99
Felicia amelloides 227, 245
forget-me-nots 52, *235*
Forsythia 132
'Lynwood' 28, *95*
suspensa 99
atrocaulis 99
sieboldii 99
foxgloves, Excelsior hybrids 57, *57*
Fremontodendron californicum 100,
101
mexicanum 100
Fritillaria 182–5, *182*, *184*
camschatcensis 182, 183
meleagris 139, *139*, 140, 183
michailovskyi 184, 185
pallidiflora 184, 185
pyrenaica 139, 183, *184*
uva-vulpis 184, 185
fritillary 143, 145, 182–5
fruit 60–1, *61*, *126*, 127–30
Fuchsia 214, 216
cultivars 227
'Thalia' *227*
Galanthus 137, 155–6
caucasicus 156
elwesii 35
nivalis 'Lutescens' *155*
Garrya elliptica 100
Gazania 142, 228
Genista 13, 28
aetnensis 20
hispanica 28, *50*
lydia 28, *31*
Gentiana asclepiadea 'Knightshayes'
46
verna angulosa 248
geranium (pelargonium) 216, *218*, 23
Geranium 'Claridge Druce' 43
endressii 'A T Johnson' 43
'Johnson's Blue' 43
psilostemon 43
sanguineum lancastriense
'Splendens' 32
Glechoma hederacea 'Variegata' 228
Gleditsia triacanthos 'Sunburst' 17
godetias 53
grape hyacinths 143, 186, 209
Grevillea robusta 228, *228*
Habranthus 143
tubispathus 192
Halimium lasianthum 100, *104*
× *Halimiocistus wintonensis* 100
Hamamelis mollis 15, 24, 25
Hebe 101, 229